QUALIFICATIONS
for
Hell or Heaven

QUALIFICATIONS *for*
Hell or Heaven

BRUCE BULLOCK

PAPERBACK: 978-1-949502-58-9
EBOOK: 978-1-949502-59-6

Ordering Information:

For orders and inquiries, please contact:
1-888-375-9818
www.toplinkpublishing.com
bookorder@toplinkpublishing.com

Printed in the United States of America

CONTENTS

Preface vii

Chapter 1:   Eternal Qualifications at Birth....................1
Chapter 2:   Infant Death 10
Chapter 3:   Rewards of Highest Qualifications........... 14
Chapter 4:   Alternative Qualifications....................... 19
Chapter 5:   God and How to Find Him.....................27
Chapter 6:   Holiness...38
Chapter 7:   Justification 52
Chapter 8:   Arrested Development............................57
Chapter 9:   Lost Sheep Found..................................65
Chapter 10: Walking 71
Chapter 11: Gifts 76
Chapter 12: Grace..86
Chapter 13: Sanctification...89
Chapter 14: Glorification 95
Chapter 15: Everlasting Covenants.............................97
Chapter 16: Forgiveness.. 118
Chapter 17: Deliverance 123
Chapter 18: Eternal Life in Resurrection 135

PREFACE

In human society we recognize a vast variety of positions, ranks, and levels of power, responsibility and authority, for each of which there are qualifications that must be met. If one does not meet the qualifications for a certain position, the apparatus of human institutions will operate to sift a person out of any higher position than he is qualified for. Though this sifting is not always effective and leaves some individuals in higher positions than they qualify for, and others who are highly qualified left behind in positions far below their abilities, the process in general places the most qualified at the top and the least qualified at the bottom.

Though there always have been unfairness, injustice and inequality involved, the human world of society tends to operate in general according to this system of qualifications. All men and women have a need to seek and strive for the best qualifications in the world in order to attain the highest positions in the world. But there is another unseen world in which man qualifies at birth without any effort on his part for one of only two positions or destinies available.

What man does not see at birth, or often after years of worldly learning and study to become better qualified, is himself and what he consists of. In childhood and youth people tend to think of themselves as their physical bodies and they tend to ignore and flee from any idea that the body might be perishable, though it invariably is. There are, however, two far more important parts of mortal man that actually do have the potential to possess the immortality that the body lacks: the soul and the spirit.

Since all men start with the erroneous notion that their bodies are their being, as they gradually discover that to be a vain hope, they learn that the soul is where their desired immortal being lies; it is in fact the seat of that desire and consists of our thoughts or intellect, our emotions and our will. No man, however, has ever found fulfillment or satisfaction in the human soul, though Buddha and his followers may have quieted and appeased it somewhat, no erudite reasoning of philosophers has ever explained it.

The third and least seen yet most important part of us, whence our very existence comes and where all of our potential destiny lies is the spirit, inseparably linked with the soul, but the only part of man that can tame and save the soul. Deluded mankind, which we all are, needs to seek understanding of itself and to discover that the world is not his destination nor his ally. Reality is utterly different from what we see or think. Eternal life, power, dominion and authority over all creation in the earth have been taken away from mankind by the deception of the devil that Adam accepted. Man's worldly reality has been thereby severed and cut off from ernal spiritual reality which consists of the will and purposes of God, manifested in his only begotten Son and our Lord Jesus Christ, who paid the price to redeem us from the serpent's kingdom of darkness and receive us into his eternal kingdom of light.

This is a work written in obedience to a word of knowledge from my pastor, and I was quick to obey and start writing. I have confined the writing as much as possible to commentary that can be substantiated by the Scriptures themselves without extensive opinions of my own. I have included some very lengthy passages of Holy Scripture in order to present the most comprehensive understanding possible of what the Holy Spirit has revealed to me about those scriptures.

Addendum to 2018 Edition

This is not a book of apologetics to convince or prove to anyone the possibility of eternal life and the way to reach it, or to prove the existence of God. I already told you where you can find all that, if you seek it. This book is a book of meat for those who already believe and are seeking more, having been saved by the milk of the Word. Yet, it is not any kind of advanced course for which you are required to have passed the milk course; all can enter seeking at any level of milk or meat and receive all there is at that level, knowing that there are attainable infinitely higher levels for eternity, which constitute your spiritual inheritance. Choice is always a factor in the level of one's spiritual inheritance

Schools that, on the other hand, are "of the world", are not analogous, though they too are divided into grades, diplomas, degrees and levels, all of which are terminated at death. Consequently, there are two different worlds in Which mankind must seek to reach the highest level, according to both the will of mankind and the will of God. All will and purposes of mankind's B.A., M.A. and PhD. are utterly empty, if not bound together with the will and purposes of the eternal God.

★★★★★★

It is essential that Judeo-Christian believers in these last days be filled with the full counsel of God, in order to fulfill Christ's great commission to preach the Gospel to the ends of the earth, and having done all to stand.

Indeed, He is coming soon, as all the signs of His coming are already manifest though still, as Jesus said, no man knows or shall know the day or the hour. So, we must remain vigilant and ready like the wise virgins.

> *Matthew 25:13*
> *"Then the kingdom of heaven shall be likened to ten virgins who took their lamps and went out to meet the bridegroom. Now five of them were wise, and five were foolish. Those who were foolish took their lamps and took no oil with them, but the wise took oil in their vessels with their lamps. But while the bridegroom was delayed, they all slumbered and slept*
> *"And at midnight a cry was heard: 'Behold, the bridegroom is coming; go out to meet him!' Then all those virgins arose and trimmed their lamps. ⁸And the foolish said to the wise, 'Give us some of your oil, for our lamps are going out But the wise answered, saying, 'No, lest there should not be enough for us and you; but go rather to those who sell, and buy for yourselves.' And while they went to buy, the bridegroom came, and those who were ready went in with him to the wedding; and the door was shut.*
> *"Afterward the other virgins came also, saying, 'Lord, Lord, open to us!' But he answered and said, 'Assuredly, I say to you, I do not know you.'*
> *"Watch therefore, for you know neither the day nor the hour in which the Son of Man is coming.*

In this book you will find some basic guidelines, admonitions and suggestions along with the many scriptural passages, but for a deeper searching of the scriptures themselves you will need to study the printed Word on the pages of the Bible and seek to see and hear the living Word that will be revealed to you as you seek. Seek and ye shall find.

Matthew 7:7
"Ask, and it will be given to you; seek, and you will find; knock, and it will be opened to you. For everyone who asks receives, and he who seeks finds, and to him who knocks it will be opened.

CHAPTER 1
Eternal Qualifications at Birth

Coming into the world every infant is endowed with the breath of life, innocence and utter dependence upon anyone who will provide care. Yet each one at that moment of Birth arrives fully qualified for certain things. The infant is not only qualified for these things, but predestined for them, namely death of its physical embodiment and eternal punishment for sin in the fires and torment of hell. Mercifully, however, each is also fully qualified to choose, when grown enough to be able, to do the will of God and have eternal life in heaven with the creator of the universe,

> *Rev.20:11-15*
> *Then I saw a great white throne and Him who sat on it, from whose face the earth and the heaven fled away. And there was found no place for them. And I saw the dead, small and great, standing before God, and books were opened. And another book was opened, which is the Book of Life. And the dead were judged according to their works, by the things which were written in the books. The sea gave up the dead who were in it, and Death and Hades delivered up the dead who were in them. And they were judged, each one according to his works. ¹⁴Then Death and Hades were cast into the lake of fire. This is the second death. And anyone not found written in the Book of Life was cast into the lake of fire.*

Many, perhaps most, who call themselves Christian are plunged into denial, doubt and speculation to extrapolate some more merciful fate for infants, imagining themselves to be far more compassionate than God whenever they hear of God's wrath or His punishment. And they react this way because of their lack of knowledge.

> *2 Thes 2:7-12*
> *For the mystery of lawlessness is already at work; only He who now restrains will do so until He is taken out of the way. And then the lawless one will be revealed, whom the Lord will consume with the breath of His mouth and destroy with the brightness of His coming. The coming of the lawless one is according to the working of Satan, with all power, signs, and lying wonders, and with all unrighteous deception among those who perish, because they did not receive the love of the truth, that they might be saved. And for this reason God will send them strong delusion, that they should believe the lie, that they all may be condemned who did not believe the truth but had pleasure in unrighteousness.*

> *Hosea 4:6*
> *My people are destroyed for lack of knowledge.*
> *Because you have rejected knowledge,*
> *I also will reject you from being priest for Me;*
> *Because you have forgotten the law of your God,*
> *I also will forget your children*

Though we all, whether believers or not, would like to dispel from our consciousness any concept of or belief in hell, yet hell is clearly and emphatically revealed in the Scriptures as the ultimate eternal abode of the devil, all his minions and of all who reject the redemption of God.

And in the scriptures, we also find revealed to us that the "fall" of man has much to do with all this, but how much? Our lack of knowledge is revealed by the fact that most of us don't know. Even many who constantly search the scriptures in the book of Genesis have overlooked the fact that God's entire plan of redemption existed long before the creation of man or anything else in the entire universe.

Isaiah 14:9-19

"Hell, from beneath is excited about you,
to meet you at your coming;
It stirs up the dead for you,
All the chief ones of the earth;
It has raised up from their thrones
All the kings of the nations.
They all shall speak and say to you:
'Have you also become as weak as we?
Have you become like us?
Your pomp is brought down to Sheol, And the
sound of your stringed instruments; The maggot
is spread under you,
And worms cover you.'
"How you are fallen from heaven, O Lucifer,
son of the morning!
How you are cut down to the ground,
You who weakened the nations!
For you have said in your heart: 'I will ascend into heaven,
I will ascend above the heights of the clouds, I will be
like the Most High.'
Yet you shall be brought down to Sheol,

"Those who see you will gaze at you, and consider you, saying:

'Is this the man who made the earth tremble,
who shook kingdoms,
Who made the world as a wilderness?
"All the kings of the nations, All of them, sleep in glory,
Everyone in his own house;
But you are cast out of your grave
Like an abominable branch,
Like the garment of those who are slain,
Thrust through with a sword,
Who go down to the stones of the pit,
Like a corpse trodden underfoot.

Ezekiel 28:2
The word of the LORD came to me again, saying,
"Son of man, say to the prince of Tyre, 'Thus says the
Lord GOD:

"Because your heart is lifted up,
And you say, 'I am a god,
I sit in the seat of gods,
In the midst of the seas,'
Yet you are a man, and not a god,
Though you set your heart as the heart of a god
(Behold, you are wiser than Daniel!
With your wisdom and your understanding, you have
gained riches for yourself,
And gathered gold and silver into your treasuries;
By your great wisdom in trade you have increased your
riches, and your heart is lifted up because of your riches),"
Therefore, thus says the Lord GOD:
"Because you have set your heart as the heart of a god,
Behold, therefore, I will bring strangers against you, The
most terrible of the nations;

*And they shall draw their swords against the beauty of
your wisdom and defile your splendor.*
*They shall throw you down into the Pit, and you shall
die the death of the slain in the midst of the seas.*
*"Will you still say before him who slays you, 'I am a god'?
But you shall be a man, and not a god, In the hand of
him who slays you.*
*You shall die the death of the uncircumcised By the
hand of aliens;*
For I have spoken," says the Lord GOD.'"

*Moreover, the word of the LORD came to me, saying, ¹² "Son of
man, take up a lamentation for the king of Tyre, and say to him,
'Thus says the Lord GOD:*

*"You were the seal of perfection, Full of wisdom and
perfect in beauty.*
*You were in Eden, the garden of God; Every precious
stone was your covering: The sardius, topaz, and
diamond, Beryl, onyx, and jasper,*
*Sapphire, turquoise, and emerald with gold. The
workmanship of your timbrels and pipes Was prepared
for you on the day you were created.*
*"You were the anointed cherub who covers; I
established you;*
You were on the holy mountain of God;
You walked back and forth in the midst of fiery stones.
*you were perfect in your ways from the day you were
created, till iniquity was found in you.*
*"By the abundance of your trading you became filled
with violence within, and you sinned;*
*Therefore, I cast you as a profane thing Out of the
mountain of God;*

And I destroyed you, O covering cherub, From the midst of the fiery stones.
"Your heart was lifted up because of your beauty; You corrupted your wisdom for the sake of your splendor; I cast you to the ground,
I laid you before kings, that they might gaze at you.
"You defiled your sanctuaries by the multitude of your iniquities,
By the iniquity of your trading;
Therefore, I brought fire from your midst;
It devoured you,
And I turned you to ashes upon the earth
In the sight of all who saw you.
All who knew you among the peoples are astonished at you; You have become a horror,
And shall be no more forever.
Then the word of the LORD came to me, saying, [21] *"Son of man, set your face toward Sidon, and prophesy against her,* [22] *and say, 'Thus says the Lord GOD:*
"Behold, I am against you, O Sidon;
I will be glorified in your midst;
And they shall know that I am the LORD,
When I execute judgments in her and am hallowed in her.
For I will send pestilence upon her, And blood in her streets;

The wounded shall be judged in her midst by the sword against her on every side; Then they shall know that I am the LORD.

"And there shall no longer be a pricking brier or a painful thorn for the house of Israel from among all who are around them, who despise them. Then they shall know that I am the Lord GOD."

'Thus says the Lord GOD: "When I have gathered the house of Israel from the peoples among whom they are scattered, and am *hallowed in them in the sight of the Gentiles, then they will dwell in their own land which I gave to My servant Jacob. And they will dwell safely there, build houses, and plant vineyards; yes, they will dwell securely, when I execute judgments on all those around them who despise them. Then they shall know that I am the LORD their God."*

> *Jude 1:6*
> *And the angels which* **kept not their first estate, but left their own habitation,** *he hath reserved in everlasting chains under darkness unto the judgment of the great day. -*

The word of the Lord that warns the kings of Tyre and Sidon speaks not to earthly kings, but to the rebellious angelic powers that usurped man's dominion and authority to corrupt all their glory through the pride and confidence that they harbored in their hatred and warfare against God's chosen nation. Though it might by now seem otherwise to the reader, I have no interest in making this a treatise on demonology or a depiction like Dante's Inferno of hell. And though there are alive today a few individuals who have seen and experienced hell and returned to bring warning of its eternal horrors,

I can only agree with that warning and try to reinforce it by pointing out that the deciding rebellion was that of Lucifer which probably did not occur in time at all but before the creation of man or any part of the universe, and God, who eternally knows the end from the beginning, had it always in his purpose to allow the rebellion and disobedience of Lucifer, Satan and Adam in order to manifest a greater miracle than creation and one second only to our redemption through His only begotten Son Jesus Christ. And that miracle second only to salvation is His establishment of choice by which alone a man can be made righteous, whole, be saved and receive eternal life. If choice had not been manifested before creation, hope could never have arisen or been found.

Among many other things, or rather among other spiritual words, that are bandied about in the world as if they were understood by the world, hope emanates from the Spirit of God alone, just as choice does. They both have their worldly or carnal counterfeits as do all holy things of God, which can only be perceived spiritually.

> *Gal 5:16-17*
> *I say then: Walk in the Spirit, and you shall not fulfill the lust of the flesh. For the flesh lusts against the Spirit, and the Spirit against the flesh; and these are contrary to one another, so that you do not do the things that you wish.*

The celestial rebel, Satan, exerts imponderably powerful efforts to conceal from mortal man any knowledge of his diabolical existence as an evil spiritual force or especially the existence in man of any other spiritual capacity available to free man from the infernal fate into which he is born. Satan delights in man's ignorance of all benevolent, sacred spiritual power that can give him new life as a new born creature with a new born spirit, that, when nurtured, can overcome all sin, death and the devil. It is Jesus Christ alone who has ever overcome sin, death and the devil and opened access for man directly to the Father. Jesus is the only way, the only truth and the only life eternal.

John 14:6
"I am the way, the truth, and the life. No one comes to
the Father except through Me.

Though God has wrath, He has been withholding it for many millennia, because God is love and is not willing that any should perish. It is the devil who seeks your destruction through any means possible, especially the means most readily available to him, your lack of knowledge.

John 10:10
The thief does not come except to steal, and to kill, and
to destroy. I have come that they may have life, and that
they may have it more abundantly.

If the devil can keep you in ignorance of that fact and of other facts revealed in the Scriptures, he succeeds in stealing not only vast amounts of the limited time of your lifespan, but also every possibility of love, joy and peace that you might have had that were always held available by God for you to choose.

CHAPTER 2
Infant Death

S ince I chose to point out the eternal horrors of hell, for which we all qualify at birth, before mentioning the infinite grace of God available to us to escape those horrors, I owe it to young parents to dispel the fears that my first chapter might have inspired in them for their children. God's wrath is not reserved for any innocent children nor even for wretched, vicious old sinners, who even at the last moment on their death beds repent, for He is not willing that any should perish, and hell is reserved for only a limited, highly qualified group, which includes only Satan, one third of the angels who rebelled with him, hell itself and death and all those who denied and rejected the risen Christ by the miraculous gift of choice, which could have saved them.

The parent who loves his or her child is by nature consumed by a need and desire to protect the child from harm of any kind. It is vital for parents to know that God's love for that child is infinitely greater than their own, and that His absolute protection is readily available when asked for, immediately when prayed for: it is not necessary to wait for a life-threatening disease or disaster to afflict the child before praying. The unborn child in the womb can be prayed for and, even if already afflicted in the womb with hereditary defects or deformity, can be changed and healed before departing from it. And even if you don't believe, the Lord has cast a hedge of protection around that innocent newborn. Scriptures in Romans, though concerned with the law and distinctions between Jew and Gentile, apply quite appropriately to infants and children of both believing and uninformed parents.

> *Romans 2:6-11*
> *—who "will render to each one according to his deeds":* *[7]eternal life to those who by patient continuance in doing good seek for glory, honor, and immortality; but to those who are self-seeking and do not obey the truth, but obey unrighteousness—indignation and wrath, tribulation and anguish, on every soul of man who does evil, of the Jew first and also of the Greek; but glory, honor, and peace to everyone who works what is good, to the Jew first and also to the Greek. [11]For there is no partiality with God.*

> *Romans 3:3-4*
> *For what if some did not believe? Will their unbelief make the faithfulness of God without effect? Certainly not! Indeed, let God be true but every man a liar. As it is written: "That, you may be justified in Your words, and may overcome when You are judged."*

Alas, your child is born into this fallen world as a sinner, and will eventually sin, but:

> *Proverbs 22:6*
> *Train up a child in the way he should go, and when he is old he will not depart from it.*

Your child is not threatened by Hell in his innocence, but as soon as sin takes hold in him, your love is insufficient to rescue him, and the child becomes responsible for working out his own redemption through God's gift of the miracle of choice. Your part then as a parent can only be to do as the proverb says and to pray for his salvation.

> *John 14:13-14*
> *And whatever you ask in My name, that I will do, that the Father may be glorified in the Son. If you ask anything in My name, I will do it'd*

> *Philippians 4:6-7*
> *Be anxious for nothing, but in everything by prayer and supplication, with thanksgiving, let your requests be made known to God; ⁷and the peace of God, which surpasses all understanding, will guard your hearts and minds through Christ Jesus.*

Where your parental love no longer suffices the infinite unconditional love of God will take over for the rest of the child's life after he has found sin and his sinful nature. The hedge of protection and the angels which protected your child at birth in the purity of his innocence will never leave your child, if your prayer in faith covers him. For parents who don't believe the lives of their children take a natural course into sin of one kind or another, from which they will have to work out their own salvation or damnation, as they choose. The way to repentance and salvation is never closed to any.

Lamentably the fate of the children of believers is the same when the protection of parental love fails and the only hope remaining for the prodigal son or daughter who rejects parental admonition is to find God on their own. It is never a parent's fault, whether believer or doubter, that a child goes astray to follow the kingdom of darkness to which we all were once enslaved. Although it grieves the heart of any parent to see his offspring fallen into crime or addiction or sexual enslavement, no parent should take upon himself the guilt of the child's sins. To do so is to fall into a favorite deception of the devil. That is not the way that a believing or unbelieving parent can help one's child in sin.

But there is a 100% effective way that a parent can provide that help, that parental love has failed to provide, and that is prayer to God, whether you believe in Him or not. When your parental distress is grave enough the Lord will provide the faith you need to believe despite all obstacles All faith is a gift of His grace and you will believe and have the faith you need when you need it and choose it. How ever bad it gets for your child, the prayer that you pray in faith believing and persist in will be answered and manifested how ever long it takes. The Prayer will never fall to the ground if diligently pursued.

CHAPTER 3
Rewards of Highest Qualifications

S ince the historical fall of Adam and Eve, which I know to be an historical event on earth in the realm of time as we know it, no further effort was ever required from any man to qualify for death and eternal torment in hell. As long as the enemy could keep us unaware of that reality and any available remedies against it, Satan too had to expend almost no effort to retain us as his slaves in bondage until he has us fully prepared to stoke his fires in hell.

There are multiple rewards and multiple ways of receiving Satan's highest rewards, many of which are revealed in Solomon's Book of Proverbs. The Lord honored both His covenant with David to place Solomon on the throne and His promised gift of wisdom to Solomon, even though both father and son transgressed grievously against the Lord. Nevertheless, his writings are indeed scripture revealed to him by the Holy Spirit, who can also reveal their wisdom to us.

Among Satan's rewards in addition to those in hell that we have already mentioned are those on earth: 1. Ill health, 2. Frequent and extended illness, Deformity, 4. Absence or defective function of limbs, sight, hearing or various organs, 5. poverty 6. abandonment by parents and guardians 6. strife, anger, 8. dementia, 9. Debt, 10 poverty, 11. delusion, ignorance, unbelief, etc. ad infinitum. The list of his miseries in this list is endless. Alas most of humanity has no idea why these dreadful things happen and is unaware of the plan and purpose of God to send his Son to redeem us all from all that. But Satan is not found under every rock and lurking behind every door, though his sole purpose is to be there whenever he can to deceive and destroy us.

> *John 10:10:*
> *The thief does not come except to steal, and to kill, and to destroy. I have come that they may have life, and that they may have it more abundantly.*

Though we all qualify for the devil's rewards from infancy onward and are destined to receive them forever both in life and death unless we find a better way, there is a better way, but only one. Because you are nice and come from a nice family and always try to do nice things and were never convicted of even a traffic violation is not the way. No public display of your piety or your good deeds or your generosity is the way either. The existence of God is obvious, as the Holy Spirit revealed to the Apostle Paul in his letter to the Romans.

> *John 1:18-21*
> *For the wrath of God is revealed from heaven against all ungodliness and unrighteousness of men, who suppress the truth in unrighteousness, because what may be known of God is manifest in them, for God has shown it to them. For since the creation of the world His invisible attributes are clearly seen, being understood by the things that are made, even His eternal power and Godhead, so that they are without excuse, because, although they knew God, they did not glorify Him*

as God, nor were thankful, but became futile in their thoughts, and their foolish hearts were darkened.

No idea, plan or scheme of mankind has ever changed or can ever change the nature or the fate of any human being; As urgent as man's need is for the better way he continues to devise a way of his own by doing things that he imagines might be pleasing to God (if he exists) and that he knows to be pleasing or at least persuasive to his fellow man, which is also not the way. Jesus, the Son of God Himself said:

John 14:6
"I am the way, the truth, and the life. No one comes to the Father except through me.

This Jesus said in response to Thomas, one of His twelve chosen disciples, who, perhaps, believed the least, (if it was not Peter himself) and not like John who loved and believed the most. Yet neither Thomas nor Peter was excluded nor was John preferred when Jesus breathed the Holy Spirit into all of them after His resurrection. Only Judas Iscariot, who had already gone to his eternal reward from Satan in hell was excluded.

Although Satan would certainly also be delighted to have you as a companion in his kingdom of darkness, he is not able alone to accomplish his purpose despite the mighty power he wields with one third of the angels of heaven, sons of God, who rebelled with him, spiritual powers far beyond those of any natural man. Yet Satan has little need to muster all his forces at once, because he has two other mighty allies who accomplish the work for him: the world and the flesh, your world and your flesh. In his rebellion before creation and his subsequent seduction of Adamic mankind he altered man's nature from an eternal spiritual being to walk in the cool of the day in the garden with God forever to a mortal creature destined to perish enslaved in his kingdom of darkness.

God, however, in addition to creating the miracle of choice and all the angels of God before creating the heavens and the earth, created redemption that, when chosen, plucks all those who believe Him out of the hand of the devil and take you to be with Him in heaven forever filled with His unconditional love, joy, peace and bounty. Only the brief span of time between birth and death of our mortal flesh, do we have to believe and receive the redemption freely offered to all flesh who will receive it from the Creator of heaven and earth, our Lord and savior Jesus Christ, who became flesh to die for our sin from which nothing else could ever save us or any whom we love.

Though most people are fond of enumerating and classifying various types of sins, in reality there is only one sin, which is doing anything that is contrary to or in defiance of the will of God, and since the fall of Adam there is only one Man who ever failed to commit that sin through a corrupted nature, and that Man is the Son of Man, who is also the Son of God and the creator of the universe, who died uncorrupted and is risen from the dead incorruptible.

If you prefer the kingdom of darkness, here are some rather certain means by which Solomon tells us we can continue to qualify.

> *Proverbs 1:24-37*
> *Because I have called and you refused, I have stretched out my hand and no one regarded, because you disdained all my counsel, and would have none of my rebuke,*

17

I also will laugh at your calamity; I will mock when your terror comes,

When your terror comes like a storm, and your destruction comes like a whirlwind, when distress and anguish come upon you.

"Then they will call on me, but I will not answer; They will seek me diligently, but they will not find me.

Because they hated knowledge and did not choose the fear of the LORD,

They would have none of my counsel and despised my every rebuke.

Therefore they shall eat the fruit of their own way and be filled to the full with their own fancies.

For the turning away of the simple will slay them, And the complacency of fools will destroy them; ³³But whoever listens to me will dwell safely, And will be secure, without fear of evil."

A powerful ally of the devil that engulfs us and blinds our eyes by its dazzle and ever-increasing pace and diversity is the world which also gluts and deafens our hearing to distract us from any consciousness of the bondage in which he holds us, or of the redeemer who can rescue us from his destructive power. But Satan's most powerful ally is the flesh, your flesh and mine, our mortal bodies that so readily lust after all the perishing things of the world and every sin of the flesh. If it seems important to you to maintain your highest qualifications for the deepest pit of hell with which you were born, do little or nothing, but if that seems unappealing, there are other sets of qualifications that you need to learn about.

CHAPTER 4
Alternative Qualifications

In human society in the world it is almost inconceivable to imagine an individual who would remain sufficiently content with his ignorance and the devil's deception to seek no other or better qualifications. The world has laws that require all children to accumulate a certain number of qualifications to reach the requirements of maturity for citizenship in society. To remain forever in Satan's spiritual realm of darkness there is nothing in the world that one has to do. But in the meantime, all of us whether we like it or not are obliged to live and linger for a certain span in a different realm, which seems no longer to be a dark spiritual realm but a physical, material realm.

By our fallen nature in the world we retain little or no consciousness of that spiritual realm of death and hell into which we have been sold by the choices of Lucifer and Adam, Without Christ we have no awareness of the spiritual realm of light and eternal life by which God has made all provision to save us from both eternal suffering in hell and diabolical deceptions of the world. In the world we live for a short time in our perishable flesh, believing most of the time erroneously that the flesh is somehow imperishable and is who and what we are, and that the world is where we belong and the only thing that we have to pursue. The devil is quite content that you should have no awareness of him and find your contentment in the world with which he is closely allied. As long as the world can entice and deceive us Satan is spared the considerable effort of doing it himself.

The world is, however, not the devil's only ally ready to assist him at all times in reinforcing his firm grip on our souls, and that ally is your flesh, the very body in which you placed all your hopes and confidence, your self. We can all choose to live our short span in pursuit of the wealth and pleasures of the world and the lusts of the flesh, but the love of God is too infinitely great to allow us simply to perish in that way,

Jesus, the creator of the universe, when he was tempted by the devil in the desert while fasting forty days and forty nights, did not contest Satan's assertion of dominion and ownership over all the kingdoms of the earth that He had created and given into the hands of Adam to have eternal dominion, authority and power, for Adam, in disobedience to the Word of God, had insouciantly really given it away into Satan's hand. Jesus indeed rebuked him with His Word, but He did not dispute Adam's tragic choice, with which God had endowed him and allowed him to make. Yet the purposes of God which He had determined before the creation of the world would not be thwarted by any error or disobedience of man or devil, and, through the inconceivable pain and suffering of His Son, Jesus Christ, He has manifested His redemption of all creation.

God never changed his eternal promises to Adam of dominion, power and authority over the earth and all its creatures, but when surrendered to Satan by Adam, He already had His plan of redemption fully prepared, though it cost Him thousands of years of profound pain in His holy heart and ultimately the death of His only begotten Son.

Similarly, God has not withdrawn his promises and power given to Satan before creation and before Satan's rebellion leading one third of God's angels of heaven. Satan still retains his beauty and powerful attraction with which he manipulates his closely allied forces: the world and the flesh.

> *Ephesians 6:12*
> *For we do not wrestle against flesh and blood, but against principalities, against powers, against the rulers of the darkness of this age against spiritual hosts of wickedness in the heavenly places.*

In the worldly realm which the devil would have you to believe is the only one, just a physical, material world with no spiritual dimension at all, Satan doesn't mind if you discover his dark spiritual realm, because by those spiritual powers he can recruit among men witches, warlocks, mediums and priests of his hellish realm to serve him as long as they are held in ignorance of God's holy spiritual realm in heaven and on earth. The earth's natural man is easily enticed and duped in his folly to delve into the occult, astrology, demons, haunted houses, séances to bring up spirits of the dead, etc, which spiritual delving is highly approved of by the devil. Those things are only a few of the media by which Satan holds men in bondage and sinks each of his servants continually deeper into his pit of hell.

This is a mighty alliance of forces that is far greater than any power of man. Every man, woman and child is helpless against those diabolic forces in his own power. Even though there is a consciousness in mankind of some kind of hunger for a god that might extricate us some unknown way from these unknown, but feared and suspected, powers. Man flails about in ignorance trying to devise his own way out of some undefined inadequacy. Religions are devised to instruct some unknown god how he should resolve our problems, and by our philosophical schemes we work out tentative solutions that require no god.

There are those of us who have searched all of time and space and history to find whether there might exist a real supernatural god or consortium of gods to resolve our dilemma. The world provides us with amazing and overwhelming institutions of both higher worldly learning and also of higher spiritual learning, where profound studies of both the physical world and the philosophies and religions of the world have been deeply probed. An integral part of all theological seminaries of various denominational stripes is the study of comparative religion. Sadly, a preponderance of those institutions has come to the following erroneous conclusions.

1. There might be a single, supreme, supernatural God, but probably there is no God.
2. He might have been the creator of the world.
3. Perhaps there is a heaven to which people can go, if they have been good people and earn it by doing good deeds.
4. If that God exists, He would never allow there to be anything as gruesome as hell. There is no hell.
5. With all that mankind has learned and achieved by the twenty first century, the quaint tales of creation in six days can no longer be believed and many

other scriptures have to be revised and edited to be reconciled with man's superior twenty first century knowledge, reason and logic.

6. Most of the scriptures are wise allegories that no longer apply today and need to be brought up to date.
7. Every one of these assertions is a lie from the pit of hell and holds most of nominally Judeo-Christian society in its grip in these last days.

> *Revelation 3:14-16*
> *"And to the angel of the church of the Laodiceans write, 'These things says the Amen, the Faithful and True Witness, the Beginning of the creation of God: "I know your works, that you are neither cold nor hot. I could wish you were cold or hot. So then, because you are lukewarm, and neither cold nor hot, I will vomit you out of My mouth. Because you say, 'I am rich, have become wealthy, and have need of nothing'—and do not know that you are wretched, miserable, poor, blind, and naked—*

But what then is this other set of qualifications that differs from both those simple, totally absent qualifications of the devil to spend eternity burning with him in his dark spiritual realm, and, on the other hand, the qualifications for success and prosperity in the physical, material realm of the world, which are numerous and as extremely simple or complex as you want to make them. Whatever level of wealth, power and success you aspire to and reach in the worldly, material realm without awareness or consideration of the spiritual realm will give you the same result in eternity.

But there is a different spiritual realm by which the plan of God, perfected before creation, overcomes both the physical or flesh realm of the world and the bleak, rebellious spiritual realm of the devil, hell and death. Satan desired to make the qualifications for his kingdom simpler than the qualifications of God to enter His kingdom of heaven, because he was certain in his ignorance and rebellion that he could convince mankind that God's requirements were too complex and unattainable. Indeed, he has succeeded in large part in planting his simpler, no-requirements plan into churches and synagogues, and there is precious little time left for the world that God, nevertheless, loves unconditionally. to repent and receive His gifts of redemption, healing and eternal life in a better place called heaven. God's eternal plan is Jesus Christ; there is no other way.

> *John 14:6*
> —*"I am the way, the truth, and the life. No one comes to the Father except through Me.*

But Satan is utterly mistaken in his attempt to make a simpler plan, for when one looks into God's plan of redemption and seeks to know God, it becomes obvious that God's qualifications that he requires are far simpler than anything man or the devil could ever devise or imagine. In Gods realm and in His perfect plan there is certain redemption and salvation for eternity that no man can ever lose, and every man is qualified for it whenever he asks, despite whatever he might have done. There is no way that any man can earn or pay for that redemption and justification that God has provided through Jesus Christ who paid for it all gave all things by His Grace to all men who believe that He is the only begotten Son of the Father who sent Him. When men do believe the first package of gifts that they receive includes at least eternal life and rebirth with a new spirit, the Holy Spirit who has made them an utterly new creature in Christ, a spiritual infant needing care and nurturing by fellow spiritual creatures who have matured and continue maturing in Christ. Once a man enters this spiritual realm, the kingdom of God, there is no power that can ever wrest him out of it, though he is in need of spiritual nurture.

> *John 17:11-12*
> *Now I am no longer in the world, but these are in the world, and I come to You. Holy Father, keep through Your name those whom You have given Me, that they may be one as We are.* ¹²*While I was with them in the world, I kept them in Your name. Those whom You gave Me I have kept; and none of them is lost except the son of perdition, that the Scripture might be fulfilled.*

When you do nothing for your soul or spirit in Satan's realm he has your eternal reward ready for you. In heaven's realm, however, when you have once received your free reward of justification and eternal life you have barely opened the wrapping on an infinite number of additional glorious gifts that God can multiply in you forever just for the asking and receiving through God's grace. The Christ has given us gratis all the qualifications that we shall ever need in heaven or earth just for believing and receiving, whereas Satan has only one reward invariably the same.

> *John 15:16*
> *You did not choose Me, but I chose you and appointed you that you should go and bear fruit, and that your fruit should remain, that whatever you ask the Father in My name He may give you.*

I hope and pray that it is not solely by my reasoning and logic in this book that you decide to choose to believe in Jesus Christ, because the kingdom of God is not accessed by man's natural reason or logic but by the supernatural revelation of the Holy Spirit through God's Word, who is spirit and who is our Lord Jesus Christ.

CHAPTER 5
God and How to Find Him

If you believe in God, but have no personal intimacy with Him, there is little rational cause for you to cling to your belief. If you do not believe in God, you too have little rational cause to seek belief. In the world you are either reasonably happy with your lot, though you most likely desire more than you have, even if you're a multi-billionaire. or you have so little that the most desirable thing for you to seek is death to end the misery. But in either state in the world you are not content. There is something quite palpably missing for both prince and pauper. It is not only the pervasive consciousness of impending death that we all attempt to repress. It is a hunger and thirst that we can neither satisfy nor repress; and that hunger and thirst is a gift from God who is seeking us and that is the only way we find Him If you are seeking Him, He sought you first.

Oh yes, He exists, and you had better lay that foolish question to rest right now, if you ever hope to find anything. God is love and He loves you, whoever you are and whatever you have done, even if you have done unspeakable things, crimes against humanity, for which you have been condemned to death or life imprisonment. Your fellow man in the world will probably never rescind your sentence or grant you amnesty. God, however, can and regularly does pardon even such offenses when asked. Then he forgives and for ever forgets them.

If that gift of hunger and thirst for righteousness has reached you and caused you to seek God, thank Him for it and let nothing stop or delay your search. If in truth you ask, you will receive, or better described. you have received and need only to make way for and await the manifestation. But how can God pardon what man can't.? God is God and not a man.

> *Numbers 23:19*
> *"God is not a man, that He should lie, nor a son of man, that He should repent.*
> *Has He said, and will He not do?*
> *Or has He spoken, and will He not make it good?*

God's glorious plan of redemption laid before creation was manifested for the universe through the birth, death and resurrection of our Lord Jesus Christ, who came to forgive and take away the sin of the world and transform natural man, born in sin, into a new creature born again into a new spiritual nature rather than the flesh dominated nature of the old natural man. Jesus on the cross took upon himself all the sin of the world and died to forgive it all and take it all away: past sin, present sin and future sin.

> *Romans 8:1-12*
> *There is therefore now no condemnation to those who are in Christ Jesus, who do not walk according to the flesh, but according to the Spirit. ²For the law of the Spirit of life in Christ Jesus has made me free from the law of sin and death. For what the law could not do in that it was weak through the flesh, God did by*

sending His own Son in the likeness of sinful flesh, on account of sin: He condemned sin in the flesh, ⁴that the righteous requirement of the law might be fulfilled in us who do not walk according to the flesh but according to the Spirit. For those who live according to the flesh set their minds on the things of the flesh, but those who live according to the Spirit, the things of the Spirit. For to be carnally minded is death, but to be spiritually minded is life and peace. Because the carnal mind is enmity against God; for it is not subject to the law of God, nor indeed can be.

So then, those who are in the flesh cannot please God. But you are not in the flesh but in the Spirit, if indeed the Spirit of God dwells in you. Now if anyone does not have the Spirit of Christ, he is not His. And if Christ is in you, the body is dead because of sin, but the Spirit is life because of righteousness. But if the Spirit of Him who raised Jesus from the dead dwells in you, He who raised Christ from the dead will also give life to your mortal bodies through His Spirit who dwells in you.

Therefore, brethren, we are debtors—not to the flesh, to live according to the flesh. For if you live according to the flesh you will die; but if by the Spirit you put to death the deeds of the body, you will live. For as many as are led by the Spirit of God, these are sons of God. For you did not receive the spirit of bondage again to fear, but you received the Spirit of adoption by whom we cry out, "Abba, Father." The Spirit Himself bears witness with our spirit that we are children of God, and if children, then heirs—heirs of God and joint heirs with Christ, if indeed we suffer with Him, that we may also be glorified together.

We search in vain, if we hope to find and know God without Jesus and the Holy Spirit whom He has sent to us. First, we must know that He is the Elohim of Genesis 1:1, the one and only living God of the universe who is a holy trinity, yet only one God, who through the Son of the Father, Jesus. sent His Holy Spirit to guide those who believe to glorification with him in His holiness. All of this blessing is His gift with your name on it, if you want it and receive it; furthermore, you may have any part of it that you are willing to ask for and receive. But only by His grace is it accessible to you, and there is no other way by which you can earn or buy it. All these gifts from God are bought and paid for by the blood of Jesus. Anything that you do in your own strength to earn and receive the innumerable gifts of God's grace will only arrest the flow coming into you of this flood of God's glory.

You yourself are the dam that can completely block that glorious flood by heeding the demands and distractions of the world and the lusts of the flesh, hoping to set your life in order first before seeking the kingdom of heaven which all the while is within you, waiting to burst forth.

> *Matthew 6:19-21*
> *"Do not lay up for yourselves treasures on earth, where moth and rust destroy and where thieves break in and steal; but lay up for yourselves treasures in heaven, where neither moth nor rust destroy and where thieves do not break in and steal. For where your treasure is, there your heart will be also.*

The thief who breaks in and steals is Satan who governs the corruption of the moth and rust and all other death and decay in the world while filling the world with attractions that appeal to the lust of the flesh. The flesh that lusts after those things of both the flesh and of the world is your flesh and my flesh enslaved by the devil to serve his purposes in our own destruction. At birth we are inextricably allied with him and hell-bound, fully qualified with no effort required of us. The devil would have us believe that the qualifications to seek the kingdom of heaven are too numerous, complex and unattainable, whereas the truth is that Jesus has fulfilled and given to all mankind all qualifications necessary to receive the highest levels of reward that heaven offers for us to inherit. Satan would make us think that heaven's many levels of inheritance that the grace of Jesus has purchased for us are too complex to pursue when his satanic rewards are so effortlessly available, But Jesus says, *"Seek and ye shall find."*

> *Matthew 7:7-8*
> *"Ask, and it will be given to you; seek, and you will find; knock, and it will be opened to you. For everyone who asks receives, and he who seeks finds, and to him who knocks it will be opened. . .*

Seek not further and you will find nothing more, but continue seeking for eternity and you will always find more well beyond infinity. If he hasn't yet completely stopped you and stolen your salvation from you, the devil hopes at least, now that he has lost you, to prevent you from receiving the fullness of your inheritance and deceive you into unwitting collaboration with his kingdom of darkness.

Rules Only Hinder

If you were raised Christian in church it is probable that you were taught a number of moral and ethical precepts, that certainly conform to the will and purposes of God. While the observance of and obedience to those precepts cannot displease God, especially if they conform to the law, the Ten Commandments that Moses brought down from the mountain top to the children of Israel. But only one man born of woman ever fulfilled that law, and He is the only one by whom you can fulfill it. But the qualifications to fulfill that law are not found in the law, but only in Him. Those rules and commandments of the law were never able to save Israel or Judah from expulsion from their Promised Land and 2,000 years of persecution in their diaspora, because none could ever keep and observe the law under that covenant that God made with Moses.

From Noah to Moses God allowed mankind to besmirch itself in godlessness without imputing sin until He chose a people to be His people and gave them a law by which to save, bless and inherit all nations and peoples of the world. Neither Israel nor the world was ever able to fulfill the law by covering sin with the blood of bulls and goats, which God knew before creation. He knew that He would have to send His only begotten Son, by whose blood alone the sin of the world could forever be taken away under a new everlasting covenant.

Only by that covenant can any man find God, and the covenant has no list of rules by which to know God. That covenant is not of this world, mere words printed on paper, for the words printed there are the living Word of God and they are Spirit, the Holy Spirit.

John 1:17
For the law was given through Moses, but grace and truth came through Jesus Christ.

John 3:36
He who believes in the Son has everlasting life; and he who does not believe the Son shall not see life, but the wrath of God abides on him."

John 5:24
Most assuredly, I say to you, he who hears My word and believes in Him who sent Me has everlasting life, and shall not come into judgment, but has passed from death into life.

John 6:63
It is the Spirit who gives life; the flesh profits nothing. The words that I speak to you are spirit, and they are life.

The natural man in us, though conscious of some inadequacy in his soul, and longing to find some god to appeal to or to worship or to find a place to worship. will never find what he seeks until he learns how to worship. And Jesus Christ is the only one who ever told mankind how to worship, when He revealed it to the Samaritan woman at the well.

John 3:23-24
But the hour is coming, and now is, when the true worshipers will worship the Father in spirit and truth; for the Father is seeking such to worship Him. God is Spirit, and those who worship Him must worship in spirit and truth."

Are there pieces to the puzzle of how to know God? Indeed there are, but they are not rules or laws or formulas or things to do or put in place first in order to earn certain rights or privileges or levels of competency. Indeed, though there are many varying levels of intimacy with and knowledge of God, there is no way to qualify for any of them by your efforts, for Christ has provided every believer with the way, the truth and the life to proceed from each level to the next: from glory to glory by faith in Him and spiritual maturation through the Holy Spirit revealing ever more of the Word of the Lord.

> *Romans 10:14*
> *How then shall they call on Him in whom they have not believed? And how shall they believe in Him of whom they have not heard? And how shall they hear without a preacher?*

Yes, it is necessary to believe, but first to know thoroughly what you believe in. And if you have not known, it is essential to have the help of someone spiritually mature to help you learn to grow into your own maturity.

> *Romans 10:17*
> *So, then faith cometh by hearing, and hearing by the word of God.*

What then must you hear? Indeed, you must hear the Word of God, but must you always hear it only from a preacher? What if you do not hear it from a preacher and have no preacher or only one who does not preach the Word of God? Almost all of you are blessed with a voice and can read it aloud for yourself in order to hear it. And what if you have no hearing? If you can read you can receive it. There is no way that you can be utterly cut off from the Word of God, even if deaf, dumb and blind. Jesus Christ has made a way for you,

> *Romans 10:8-9*
> *"The word is near you, in your mouth and in your heart" (that is, the word of faith which we preach): that if you confess with your mouth the Lord Jesus and believe in your heart that God has raised Him from the dead, you will be saved. For with the heart one believes unto righteousness, and with the mouth confession is made unto salvation.*

So, among other things we have found the way to salvation, but salvation from what? Is it salvation only from hell, and do we now know God? Thank God that by believing in your heart and confessing in public with your mouth you are indeed saved from Satan's eternal abode, but if that is all that you have and are content with receiving no more, turning away from your new born spirit man back to your old flesh man, you have not yet known God or tasted the riches of His Glory. Though you are assured that at the death of your perishable physical body your immortal soul will be eternally alive with Christ in heaven, if you seek God no further, however, you deprive yourself by your choice of a massive spiritual inheritance promised since the foundation of the earth that surpasses all human imagination. And it is all yours for the asking, which is the process of receiving the best inheritance.

Thus, we learn that through God's miracle of choice and the grace of the Lord Jesus Christ we have already beforehand received many gifts, but after receiving His salvation we have acquired access to all things.

> *John 3:1-6*
> *There was a man of the Pharisees named Nicodemus, a ruler of the Jews.*
> *This man came to Jesus by night and said to Him, "Rabbi, we know that You are a teacher come from God; for no one can do these signs that You do unless God is with him."*
> *Jesus answered and said to him, "Most assuredly, I say to you, unless one is Born again, he cannot see the kingdom of God."*
> *Nicodemus said to Him, "How can a man be born when he is old? Can he enter a second time into his mother's womb and be born?"*
> *Jesus answered, "Most assuredly, I say to you, unless one is born of water and the Spirit, he cannot enter the kingdom of God.*
> *That which is born of the flesh is flesh, and that which is born of the Spirit is spirit.*

Without belief and the declaration of it man remains flesh that has no life and no hope of seeing the kingdom of God and certainly no eternal life. He remains lost in Satan's kingdom of darkness. Nicodemus did indeed receive that revelation and turned from being a high ranking blind leader of the blind to faith in the Word of God and his own rebirth.

> *1 Corinthians 15:20-28*
> *But now Christ is risen from the dead and has become the first fruits of those who have fallen asleep. For since by man came death, by Man also came the resurrection*

of the dead. For as in Adam all die, even so in Christ all shall be made alive. But each one in his own order: Christ the firstfruits, afterward those who are Christ's at His coming. Then comes the end, when He delivers the kingdom to God the Father, when He puts an end to all rule and all authority and power. For He must reign till He has put all enemies under His feet. The last enemy that will be destroyed is death. ²⁷For "He has put all things under His feet." But when He says "all things are put under Him," it is evident that He who put all things under Him is excepted. ²⁸Now when all things are made subject to Him, then the Son Himself will also be subject to Him who put all things under Him, that God may be all in all.

Our only limit in Christ is the one we choose, and there is never a reason to cease our spiritual growth until we are wholly in Him and all things are put under Him and made subject to Him and the Son Himself is put under the Father with us in Him and Him in the Father, that God may be all in all.

CHAPTER 6
Holiness

G od established the nation of Israel, which He promised long before it existed to Abraham and later to Isaac and to Jacob, whom He renamed Israel, after whom the land is named. And they were to be His people and He was to be their God. To Moses He gave laws and statutes by which to serve Him and fulfill His will for him, and He said:

> *Leviticus 11:44*
> *For I am the LORD your God. You shall therefore consecrate yourselves, and you shall be holy; for I am holy.*

In the conquered land of Canaan that God gave to Israel the Lord found only few men after His own heart and none that were holy But the Lord had spoken and will not be denied. Therefore, God manifested His plan laid down before the foundation of the earth to raise up out of Judah a sinless Savior to take away the sin of the world and create the only way for Israel and all mankind to become holy as He is holy by His grace through faith in Him.

> *1 Corinthians 15:20-28*
> *But now Christ is risen from the dead and has become the firstfruits of those who have fallen asleep. For since by man came death, by Man also came the resurrection*

of the dead. For as in Adam all die, even so in Christ all shall be made alive. But each one in his own order: Christ the firstfruits, afterward those who are Christ's at His coming. Then comes the end, when He delivers the kingdom to God the Father, when He puts an end to all rule and all authority and power. For He must reign till He has put all enemies under His feet. The last enemy that will be destroyed is death. For "He has put all things under His feet." But when He says "all things are put under Him," it is evident that He who put all things under Him is excepted. Now when all things are made subject to Him, then the Son Himself will also be subject to Him who put all things under Him, that God may be all in all.

Holiness is the pinnacle spiritual level that Jesus asks us to reach for, and He neither lies to us that it will be easy nor deceives us, as does the devil that it is too difficult and unattainable to be worth seeking. Satan would have us believe that his way is easier, demanding no qualifications.

Matthew 7:13
"Enter by the narrow gate; for wide is the gate and broad is the way that leads to destruction, and there are many who go in by it. Because narrow is the gate and difficult is the way which leads to life, and there are few who find it.

Jesus Christ is the truth, and the truth of the matter is that at the starting gate He has told us the gate is narrow and the way difficult. He, however is both the gate and the way that fulfills all of the qualification for each of the spiritual levels that we must reach to become with Him in God all in all.

Jesus has already traversed every one of the difficult steps of the way for us. Therefore, there is no step of the way that He has not overcome for us with greater and greater gifts at the end of each step.

Though the devil would have you believe it to be too difficult and complex even to take the first step on the path to righteousness, the glorious rewards of that step are so great that that same devil can readily convince you that there is nothing more, if you let him. God in His same infinite mercy will let you catch your breath after you have been justified by His salvation, but he desires that you should then receive more. And once you have received more from Hin and reached a higher level He still has more and forever again more whenever you ask.

None of the difficulty of the way comes from God; it comes rather from your camouflaged and concealed enemies: the world, the flesh and the devil.

> *Ephesians 6:12*
> *For we do not wrestle against flesh and blood, but against principalities, against powers, against the rulers of the darkness of this age, against spiritual hosts of wickedness in the heavenly places. Therefore, take up the whole armor of God, that you may be able to withstand in the evil day, and having done all, to stand.*

Those dark spiritual forces that we fight, though far mightier than we are, have been defeated two thousand years ago on the cross by the love and blood of Jesus, against which none of them can stand.

1 John 4:18
There is no fear in love; but perfect love casts out fear,
because fear involves torment. But he who fears has not
been made perfect in love. We love Him because He
first loved us.

Perfect love is what you received when you believed. Jesus poured it into you who are to be a vessel filled with it to pour it out to the world. There is in God no imperfect love or other imperfection. The only love that natural man without Christ ever had was a corruption of the perfect love with which God created us before Adam's fall. But when we receive Jesus' justification and salvation He also makes that perfect love available for us to pour out in his name and cast out all fear, for He loved us first.

The Lord has given us invincible spiritual defensive and offensive weapons to wield against the enemy. His love, however is the mightiest of them, against which no obstacle or enemy can stand, physical or spiritual. whenever we call upon it.

Ephesians 6:10-20
Finally, my brethren, be strong in the Lord and in the
power of His might. Put on the whole armor of God,
that you may be able to stand against the wiles of the
devil. For we do not wrestle against flesh and blood, but
against principalities, against powers, against the rulers
of the darkness of this age, against spiritual hosts of
wickedness in the heavenly places. Therefore take up the
whole armor of God, that you may be able to withstand
in the evil day, and having done all, to stand. Stand
therefore, having girded your waist with truth, having
put on the breastplate of righteousness, [15]and having

> *shod your feet with the preparation of the gospel of peace;*
> *above all, taking the shield of faith with which, you will*
> *be able to quench all the fiery darts of the wicked one.*
> *And take the helmet of salvation, and the sword of the*
> *Spirit, which is the word of God; praying always with*
> *all prayer and supplication in the Spirit, being watchful*
> *to this end with all perseverance and supplication for all*
> *the saints— and for me, that utterance may be given to*
> *me, that I may open my mouth boldly to make known*
> *the mystery of the gospel, for which I am an ambassador*
> *in chains; that in it I may speak boldly, as I ought to*
> *speak.*

If you are a new believer or arrested in your spiritual growth, the many pieces of armor and the things we have to do by faith can make it seem to be too hard or complicated, as the devil would have you think: "too many qualifications for you ever to meet; You'll never be worthy; I'm not ready for that; There's plenty of time before I have to think about heaven and hell, if there is any." But the devil is a liar and the father of liars. What we must know to save our inheritance is that Jesus has supplied you with all of the armor and all of the qualifications required for each higher step toward holiness. And if you lack anything, ask and you will receive it

With the sword of the spirit in hand, which is the Word of God, God has the greatest weapons ready for you in the baptism of the Holy Spirit through which God Himself can pray the perfect prayer through you concerning anything in the universe that God needs to have you pray for, whether you know anything about it or not. The prayer in the Spirit is prayer in the perfect will of God spoken in unknown tongues of men or angels. This prayer is available to you and under your control whenever you desire it. And it is never forced upon you. But other precious gifts come with the baptism of the Holy Spirit as the Spirit wills.

> *1 Corinthians 12:4-12*
> *There are diversities of gifts, but the same Spirit. There are differences of ministries, but the same Lord. And there are diversities of activities, but it is the same God who works all in all. But the manifestation of the Spirit is given to each one for the profit of all: for to one is given the word of wisdom through the Spirit, to another the word of knowledge through the same Spirit, to another faith by the same Spirit, to another gifts of healings by the same Spirit, to another the working of miracles, to another prophecy, to another discerning of spirits, to another different kinds of tongues, to another the interpretation of tongues. But one and the same Spirit works all these things, distributing to each one individually as He wills.*

The inestimable value of the Holy Spirit and His gifts of the spirit have the power to make you the hands and feet and voice of the living Lord Jesus Christ, who told His disciples:

> *John 14:12-14*
> **"Most assuredly, I say to you, he who believes in Me, the works that I do he will do also; and greater works than these he will do, because I go to My Father. And whatever you ask in My name, that I will do, that the Father may be glorified in the Son. [14]If you ask] anything in My name, I will do it.**

The universal church, which is His body, has not sufficiently embraced these promises, and will soon have to face its shortcomings, each congregation according to its deeds. Jesus Himself writes admonitions for the congregations.

> *Revelation 2:1-29 & 3:1-22*
> *To the angel of the church of Ephesus write,*
> *'These things say He who holds the seven stars in His right hand, who walks in the midst of the seven golden lampstands: ² "I know your works, your labor, your patience, and that you cannot bear those who are evil. And you have tested those who say they are apostles and are not and have found them liars; ³and you have persevered and have patience and have labored for My name's sake and have not become weary. ⁴Nevertheless I have this against you, that you have left your first love. ⁵Remember therefore from where you have fallen; repent and do the first works, or else I will come to you quickly and remove your lampstand from its place—unless you repent. ⁶But this you have, that you hate the deeds of the Nicolaitans, which I also hate.*
> *"He who has an ear, let him hear what the Spirit says to the churches. To him who overcomes I will give to eat from the tree of life, which is in the midst of the Paradise of God."'*

The Persecuted Church

> ⁸*"And to the angel of the church in Smyrna write,*
> ⁹*'These things says the First and the Last, who was dead, and came to life:*
> *"I know your works, tribulation, and poverty (but you are rich); and I know the blasphemy of those who say*

*they are Jews and are not but are a synagogue of Satan.
¹⁰Do not fear any of those things which you are about
to suffer. Indeed, the devil is about to throw some of you
into prison, that you may be tested, and you will have
tribulation ten days. Be faithful until death, and I will
give you the crown of life.
¹¹"He who has an ear, let him hear what the Spirit says
to the churches. He who overcomes shall not be hurt by
the second death."'*

The Compromising Church

*¹²"And to the angel of the church in Pergamos write,
'These things say He who has the sharp two-edged
sword: ¹³"I know your works, and where you dwell,
where Satan's throne is. And you hold fast to My
name and did not deny My faith even in the days in
which Antipas was My faithful martyr, who was killed
among you, where Satan dwells. ¹⁴But I have a few
things against you, because you have there those who
hold the doctrine of Balaam, who taught Balak to put a
stumbling block before the children of Israel, to eat things
sacrificed to idols, and to commit sexual immorality.
¹⁵Thus you also have those who hold the doctrine of the
Nicolaitans, which thing I hate. ¹⁶Repent, or else I will
come to you quickly and will fight against them with the
sword of My mouth.
¹⁷"He who has an ear, let him hear what the Spirit says
to the churches. To him who overcomes I will give some
of the hidden manna to eat. And I will give him a white
stone, and on the stone a new name written which no
one knows except him who receives it."'*

The Corrupt Church

[18] "And to the angel of the church in Thyatira write, 'These things says the Son of God, who has eyes like a flame of fire, and His feet like fine brass: [19] "I know your works, love, service, faith, and your patience; and as for your works, the last are more than the first. [20]Nevertheless I have a few things against you, because you allow that woman Jezebel, who calls herself a prophetess, to teach and seduce My servants to commit sexual immorality and eat things sacrificed to idols. [21]And I gave her time to repent of her sexual immorality, and she did not repent. [22]Indeed I will cast her into a sickbed, and those who commit adultery with her into great tribulation, unless they repent of their deeds. [23]I will kill her children with death, and all the churches shall know that I am He who searches the minds and hearts. And I will give to each one of you according to your works.

"Now to you I say, and] to the rest in Thyatira, as many as do not have this doctrine, who have not known the depths of Satan, as they say, I will[i] put on you no other burden. [25]But hold fast what you have till I come. [26]And he who overcomes, and keeps My works until the end, to him I will give power over the nations—
[27]'He shall rule them with a rod of iron;

They shall be dashed to pieces like the potter's vessels'—
as I also have received from My Father; [28]and I will give him the morning star.
[29] "He who has an ear, let him hear what the Spirit says to the churches.'"

The Dead Church

"And to the angel of the church in Sardis write,
These things says He who has the seven Spirits of God
and the seven stars: "I know your works, that you
have a name that you are alive, but you are dead. ²Be
watchful, and strengthen the things which remain, that
are ready to die, for I have not found your works perfect
before God. ³Remember therefore how you have received
and heard; hold fast and repent. Therefore, if you will
not watch, I will come upon you as a thief, and you will
not know what hour I will come upon you. ⁴You have
a few names even in Sardis who have not defiled their
garments; and they shall walk with Me in white, for
they are worthy. ⁵He who overcomes shall be clothed in
white garments, and I will not blot out his name from
the Book of Life; but I will confess his name before My
Father and before His angels.
⁶"He who has an ear, let him hear what the Spirit says
to the churches."'

The Faithful Church

⁷"And to the angel of the church in Philadelphia write,
⁸"These things says He who is holy, He who is true,
"He who has the key of David, He who opens and no
one shuts, and shuts and no one opens":
"I know your works. See, I have set before you an
open door, and no one can shut it; for you have a little
strength, have kept My word, and have not denied My
name. ⁹Indeed I will make those of the synagogue of
Satan, who say they are Jews and are not, but lie—
indeed I will make them come and worship before your
feet, and to know that I have loved you. ¹⁰Because

*you have kept My command to persevere, I also will
keep you from the hour of trial which shall come upon
the whole world, to test those who dwell on the earth.
¹¹Behold, I am coming quickly! Hold fast what you
have, that no one may take your crown. ¹²He who
overcomes, I will make him a pillar in the temple of
My God, and he shall go out no more. I will write on
him the name of My God and the name of the city of
My God, the New Jerusalem, which comes down out
of heaven from My God. And I will write on him My
new name.*

¹³*"He who has an ear, let him hear what the Spirit says
to the churches."*

The Lukewarm Church

¹⁴*"And to the angel of the church of the Laodiceans
write, 'These things says the Amen, the Faithful
and True Witness, the Beginning of the creation
of God: ¹⁵"I know your works, that you are
neither cold nor hot. I could wish you were cold
or hot. ¹⁶So then, because you are lukewarm, and
neither cold nor hot, I will vomit you out of My
mouth. ¹⁷Because you say, 'I am rich, have become
wealthy, and have need of nothing'—and do not
know that you are wretched, miserable, poor, blind,
and naked—¹⁸I counsel you to buy from Me gold
refined in the fire, that you may be rich; and white
garments, that you may be clothed, that the shame
of your nakedness may not be revealed; and anoint
your eyes with eye salve, that you may see. ¹⁹As
many as I love, I rebuke and chasten. Therefore,
be zealous and repent. ²⁰Behold, I stand at the door
and knock. If anyone hears My voice and opens the*

> *door, I will come in to him and dine with him, and he with Me.* ^{21}*To him who overcomes I will grant to sit with Me on My throne, as I also overcame and sat down with My Father on His throne.* ^{22}*"He who has an ear, let him hear what the Spirit says to the churches."'"*

These are historical churches that existed in Asia Minor, but they represent the types of churches that exist today as the body of Christ, and they have almost all fallen far short of the glory of God and His holiness, and there is little time left before His coming. But all those who believe shall indeed be made holy according to the will and purpose of God before creation. We must repent and confidently seek His holiness. The admonition in these seven letters extend not only to the churches institutionally, but to every man woman and child in the churches, to their families, to their governments and entire societies where the shortcomings warned of persist without repentance.

I quote these seven letters in their entirety because these are the end times into which the Lord will soon return to snatch up his church to be with Him in heaven for 1,000 years before returning again to reign and rule forever as Lord of lords and King of kings. There are elements of the failings of these churches in each believer, and those of us who fail to overcome simply won't be caught up in the rapture with Him but will have to remain behind for the reign of the Antichrist, the false prophet, the beast and their terrible tribulation.

Jesus's letter to the Ephesians identifies a spiritually mature entity, either an individual or an institution that functioned in the world efficiently but lost its initial ardent zeal and passion for the Lord and His salvation, outwardly thriving, but inwardly waning in the love with which it started. Such waning of love, although it will never take away eternal salvation it does permit the devil to steal part of our earthly peace and joy and our heavenly inheritance. Satan, of course, gains absolutely nothing in stealing from you other than his delight at your loss. We have all suffered from such losses, but by our timely repentance the Lord will restore it all to us.

In the case of those who are persecuted like the church at Smyrna in countries and situation s where they are constantly under threat of arrest, torture or death and even false doctrine from within their own ranks, those who stand firm and overcome risk no loss of inheritance. On the contrary their inheritance will only increase as they stand.

The churches and the souls that have persisted in the midst of hell's worldly domain of crime ridden neighborhoods, corruption filled countries and cesspools of sexual immorality by compromising with those conditions will never be utterly cut off from salvation. They will, however, forfeit all hope of a rich inheritance. Only repentance and return to persevere and overcome can restore part or even all of that inheritance through Jesus Christ our Lord.

The church or soul that has blessed works in abundance and increasing, genuine love of Christ in the heart (not mere natural affection), faith to persevere by the grace of God, and infinite patience like the church at Thyatyra must also overcome by casting out the corruption that it has allowed to cohabit in its sanctuary. The corruption is of several kinds: the sale of salvation, the usurping and abuse of authority and the clandestine practice and protection of sexual immorality. Historically accusations of such corruption have been leveled at the Roman Catholic Church in a finger pointing game by multiple denominations and persons who practice the same spiritual whoredom. Without repentance terrible tribulation awaits, though life eternal will not be taken away, much inheritance will be lost.

For those, like the church of Philadelphia, who faithfully love their brothers and sisters according to the Lord's command and keep by the grace of Christ all His everlasting covenants and cling to the root of the vine into which they have been grafted and also exerted all efforts to help dead branches pruned out to be grafted back in, they shall have their crowns and enter His temple as pillars with His new name and the name of His holy city coming down from heaven, the new Jerusalem, written upon them.

For Those who, like the church at Laodicea, have died spiritually in a congregation of feigned fellowship void of the love or the Holy Spirit of God, there still remains open a door for repentance by which eternal life can be precariously be retained. Perhaps by a much belated death bed repentance some tiny portion of God's potentially glorious and limitless inheritance might be available to you, but at least your eternal entrance to heaven will be assured. It really does not pay to wait that long to find out.

CHAPTER 7

Justification

The three most important steps or levels of your walk with God in the Holy Spirit and no longer in the flesh are:

1. Being made righteous by your repentance of sin, and God's gracious forgiveness, receiving in your heart Jesus Christ as Lord and savior of your life, and becoming the righteousness of God. You receive with your salvation not only forgiveness and Justification but also eternal life and the Holy Spirit and a new birth as a new creature no longer under the power of Satan, sin and death.

2. When born again you are at the threshold of heaven inside the gate as a spiritual infant in need of nurture in order to grow into spiritual maturity, which is a process called sanctification. There are countless steps and levels of sanctification, different for each individual according to the will of the Holy Spirit and what you ask Him for.in the will of God. Your new spiritual creature now has the mind of Christ by which to manifest your sanctification, sanctification that your old flesh man could never reach without Christ.

3. The goal of your sanctification is to attain to full glorification as a brother and fellow heir with Jesus

Christ. That is the high calling that He has bought for us by his death on the cross and His resurrection from the dead. No natural man who walks in the flesh will ever see that glory even in glory there are probably even higher levels to reach though I don't know what they are.

And the choices are different for every individual. God has the perfect plan for your life, if and when you ask and receive it. But don't accept any gospel from anybody who tries to tell you anything other than the full counsel of God. You will know the false prophets by their fruits and by the scriptures that they declare to be obsolete, no longer valid for the modern world, or that following their updated gospel will get you into heaven when you die and remove all trouble and tribulation from your life. That is the very lie that Satan in the snake told to Adam and Eve in the garden. The gospel of Jesus Christ says quite the contrary and gives not only gifts of His grace, but also abundant proof of His word to all who believe.

Indeed, man lives not by bread alone nor by proof alone but by faith in every living word of God. Eternal life can be found and grasped and clung to for all time and eternity in only a few words of the scripture, a verse or two. But though a few are content with just that, how or why could anyone neglect, ignore or reject the rest of His endless riches in the glory of His inheritance? The persecution and tribulation that Jesus told us we would have, with which Satan and the world would like to frighten you away from seeking salvation, are nothing in comparison to eternal fires of hell that the devil offers instead.

Isaiah 28-13
But the word of the LORD was to them, Precept upon
precept upon precept, Line upon line, line upon line,
here a little, there a little, that they might go and fall
backward, and be broken and snared and caught.

As Isaiah said, not all things come at once or immediately break off the natural flesh man from the newborn spiritual creature in the new believer and the way it works. And the order of lines and precepts little by little varies from one person to the next according to the will of the Spirit and the individual's readiness to receive. Although salvation and justification are received immediately as soon as you truly believe in your heart and declare it with your mouth, even if you don't yet know anything about it, the rest of the steps to sanctification, Glorification and holiness can only be manifested in you by the Lord Himself and not by your intellectual effort, your emotion or fervent desire, or your adherence to any law or rule other than love.

The wisdom and knowledge to hold onto the seed that you receive and nurture it to maturity to produce fruit unto sanctification you must be tenaciously persistent in prayer for revelation of the Word.to form in you a firm, unshakable foundation. No measure of your zeal will produce any fruit of the spirit in you with a lack of word in you for a shortage of time, waning of interest or other distractions. Millions have imagined themselves to be saved by accepting intellectually that Jesus is the Son of God crucified and risen from the dead but have no further knowledge of God than what they have once been told in Sunday school and never read the Bible or had revelation of any of its scriptures. Those people delude themselves and are far closer to Satan than to God, though they may be very nice people,

> *1 Peter 1:4-9*
> *Blessed be the God and Father of our Lord Jesus Christ, who according to His abundant mercy has begotten us again to a living hope through the resurrection of Jesus Christ from the dead, ⁴to an inheritance incorruptible and undefiled and that does not fade away, reserved in heaven for you, ⁵who are kept by the power of God through faith for salvation ready to be revealed in the last time.*
> *⁶In this you greatly rejoice, though now for a little while, if need be, you have been grieved by various trials, ⁷that the genuineness of your faith, being much more precious than gold that perishes, though it is tested by fire, may be found to praise, honor, and glory at the revelation of Jesus Christ, ⁸whom having not seen you love. Though now you do not see Him, yet believing, you rejoice with joy inexpressible and full of glory, ⁹receiving the end of your faith—the salvation of your souls.*
>
> *1 Peter 2:1*
> *Therefore, laying aside all malice, all deceit, hypocrisy, envy, and all evil speaking, ²as newborn babes, desire the pure milk of the word, that you may grow thereby, ³if indeed you have tasted that the Lord is gracious.*
>
> *James 4:2-3*
> *You lust and do not have. You murder and covet and cannot obtain. You fight and war. Yet you do not have because you do not ask. ³You ask and do not receive, because you ask amiss, that you may spend it on your pleasures*

Hebrews 5:13-14
For though by this time you ought to be teachers, you need someone to teach you again the first principles of the oracles of God; and you have come to need milk and not solid food. ¹³For everyone who partakes only of milk is unskilled in the word of righteousness, for he is a babe. ¹⁴But solid food belongs to those who are of full age, that is, those who by reason of use have their senses exercised to discern both good and evil.

Most of us who claim to be Christian are still feeding ourselves on milk, and when hungry return for more milk. By so doing we dishonor the work of Jesus on the cross attempting to secure our justification and salvation that Jesus has already bought for us by his blood instead of passing beyond that point to lay up the treasures in heaven of sanctification. The more often that we lapse back into the sin of the flesh that He has taken away and forgiven and cast into the sea of forgetfulness and return for more milk, the fewer treasures we lay up for ourselves in our inheritance in heaven. However, by persisting in seeking the fullness of our sanctification, the greater our inheritance in heaven grows by reason of use. There is not and never shall be through all eternity a shortage of solid spiritual food, and if we do not seek it, we shall not receive it or our greater inheritance.

Once you have believed in your heart and confessed with your mouth you will never lose your salvation, but without seeking further you will indeed lose (or more precisely abandon) much of your glorious inheritance and halt the process of your glorification in holiness. And it is all yours only through Jesus Christ our Lord and Savior by your choice.

CHAPTER 8
Arrested Development

This author at 84 years of age can tell you much about the urgency of not delaying the acquisition of your heavenly inheritance, because he has done so for decades. Only at about age 78 did he resume seeking profoundly more solid spiritual food to glorify God and thus pursue his inheritance and his own glorification through Jesus Christ. This chapter is clearly a confession of decades of drifting into apostasy, error (sin) and neglect of his inheritance. I shall abandon the third person and tell it in the first person.

Addendum to Second 2018 Edition

Now, seven years later, at 91, having ceased backsliding and intensified seeking, I have continued without limit to find spiritual growth toward a glorious inheritance in heaven.

In my youth by the grace of God, though I had never found God or known which god to seek, God gave me many gifts for which I never thanked Him, and He always had his hand on me, because He loved me as He loves you and all others in His creation. In childhood I was free, as you also are, to make any choice that I might decide upon. My loving parents attempted to lead me toward religion in a church that my mother frequented but with little support from my father.

Nevertheless, I retained enough snippets of scripture in memory to become a seeker of God, or rather of some god that might be real and capable of at least some of the miraculous things that I had heard about in church. I did not believe signs and wonders in Christianity, because I had never seen anybody in any nominally Christian church call upon, seek or manifest any miracle, Consequently, though I felt a deep hunger in my heart for God, I diligently sought Him in all the wrong places.

Though I know it now, I did not have any inkling then that Jesus had His hand on me to shield me from countless evils that pursued me from the devil, and to many of which I yielded in my sinful nature, as we have all done before repenting and receiving Christ. I led a rather directionless child's life until age 10 or 11, finding a couple of undertakings that interested me and kept me somewhat though not entirely out of trouble such as model airplane building and, in emulation of my older brother, woodworking and automobile mechanics.

Despite my ignorance of the Lord's holy hedge of protection over me to the age of eleven when I had never yet acknowledged Jesus nor thanked Him nor asked Him for anything, He started to pour out blessings upon me, for which I had never yet thanked Him. I even denied Him because nobody had informed me that His glorious, miraculous powers still prevailed undiminished and could be accessed through Him and no other way.

Jesus placed Himself in my path as the stumbling stone over which I could never pass until He found me and I found Him. Already when I was only eleven years old, He opened up a career path in music for me that far exceeded anything that I could dream of reaching without His favor. He enabled me to select the oboe as the instrument ordained for me and, against all hope to take lessons from one of the greatest oboists despite the inability of my parents, just emerging from the abject poverty of the great depression of the nineteen twenties and thirties. to pay for any kind of lessons or any instrument. I learned on a defective school instrument that was later given to me by the grace of God.

His grace and no merit of my own found me a scholarship to the National Music Camp in Michigan before I had any lessons, and where I learned that I was a miserable oboist in dire need of lessons. The Lord, still without thanks or acknowledgement, continued to bless me with rapid improvement and opportunities to play in orchestras and situation that my limited means would never have provided, including organizing performance of many solo and chamber concerts, performance while in the service with many different civic and college symphony orchestras in Massachusetts. The service also blessed me with the G.I. bill which not only provided me with a college education but sent me to Europe for nearly seven years for a good part of it. While in Europe God's grace placed me in the chair of principle oboist in one of the world's most renowned orchestras at the Salzburg festival in Austria.

Finally, still ignorant of Christ's salvation and seeking in various creeds and cults for a miraculous god or manifestation, I became quite ill and was persuaded to return to the United States and decided to reside in New Mexico rather than my native Minnesota. Very soon though, the Lord led me to seek the miraculous in California, where I finally found not only that for which I sought many years in unrepentant arrogance, but I finally found Him, who had favored me without my thanks for twenty-seven years. And He rewarded me with a glorious Pauline Damascus road revelation and anointing. . . As a babe in Christ I hungered to go further in the Lord and receive both water baptism and baptism in the Holy Spirit.

Lamentably, as a newborn babe in Christ, under attack from Satan who had lost me, I began to drift away from the voice of God and make a few of my own erroneous decisions and choices.

> *"Therefore, hear the parable of the sower: [19]When anyone hears the word of the kingdom, and does not understand it, then the wicked one comes and snatches away what was sown in his heart. This is he who received seed by the wayside. [20]But he who received the seed on stony places, this is he who hears the word and immediately receives it with joy; [21]yet he has no root in himself but endures only for a while. For when tribulation or persecution arises because of the word, immediately he stumbles. [22]Now he who received seed among the thorns is he who hears the word, and the cares of this world and the deceitfulness of riches choke the word, and he becomes unfruitful. [23]But he who received seed on the good ground is he who hears the word and understands it, who indeed bears fruit and produces: some a hundredfold, some sixty, some thirty*

Though I had been somewhat familiar with this parable all my life, I had never yet understood it clearly. But Satan knows that scripture as well as I did, even better. And he began immediately after I had received the Lord as my Savior to employ that parable to take me back into his kingdom of darkness but in reverse order. Although he also knows that patience is a fruit of the Spirit of God, he knew that he would have to feign decades of patience, even though his time is short, in order to entice and deceive me enough to cause my fall from grace. But when we have received the Lord there is nothing that the devil can do to us unless we allow him to do it

The devil knew that the seed had been sown into my good soil and that I had been sealed by the Holy Spirit in eternal life, and he had no way of starting his attack there. But by the previous point of the parable he knew that he could begin. He knew that he could cause me to misinterpret 1 *Corinthians 7:17-24:*

But as God has distributed to each one, as the Lord has called each one, so let him walk. And so I ordain in all the churches. ¹⁸Was anyone called while circumcised? Let him not become uncircumcised. Was anyone called while uncircumcised? Let him not be circumcised. ¹⁹Circumcision is nothing and uncircumcision is nothing, but keeping the commandments of God is what matters. ²⁰Let each one remain in the same calling in which he was called. ²¹Were you called while a slave? Do not be concerned about it; but if you can be made free, rather use it. ²²For he who is called in the Lord while a slave is the Lord's freedman. Likewise, he who is called while free is Christ's slave. ²³You were bought at a price; do not become slaves of men. ²⁴Brethren, let each one remain with God in that state in which he was called.

There are so many profound things for a young new believer to contemplate in those verses all at once that it can and will be overwhelming, if one does not "wait on the Lord" to sort it all out. Satan easily made me think that I had to hurry pursuing my musical career which unbeknown to me had become my idol by which to glorify myself rather than God. The devil knew that that is a common path followed by many musicians and artists of every discipline whose art is a gift of God that can be anointed for the glorification of God as well as a curse destructive to the self.

Next, among my other cares of this world besides employment to earn my bread, the devil duped me to believe that when I left California where I had travelled to find the miraculous there could be no Spirit filled congregation in Albuquerque, New Mexico or elsewhere preaching the full council of God, and that I would find only my own prayer in the Spirit to sustain me in Christ. And indeed I was stupid enough to assume that. However. Soon the Lord led me into a long lasting close loving relationship with a Christian family in music ministry, but rejecting such manifestations as speaking in tongues and the gifts of the spirit. . . In their youth they had come out of churches that practiced such things, but in the chaotic disorder that the apostle Paul warned against in the fourteenth chapter of 1 Corinthians. These friends introduced me to one of their choir members, recently divorced from an adulterous husband with two young sons to raise, and they suggested that she and I might make a good match; I was open to the suggestion but had to pray about it. And I did pray long and fervently about it. Then, alas, I made one of the worst decisions of my life without waiting for the Lords answer and entered into an eight year long marriage where I did not belong. And all I can say is mea culpa, mea maxima culpa.

Though Satan had managed to lead me astray and to sin in various ways, he had not yet extinguished my faith, and the Lord continued to bless me despite my folly, and He had kept for me my real wife whom I should have married fourteen years earlier. She loved me and was completely supportive of my faith, my aspirations, hopes and dreams and she enabled me to achieve my highest worldly ambition to found, and conduct an opera company into which we poured all our strength and substance. But we did it all in our own strength and intellectual convictions and that is where Satan found his point of attack. Though I could rant about all the forces lined up against us and, of course, did so, my ranting contributed only to a series of disasters that I had allowed the devil to accomplish. We prayed, believed and worked very hard, but not together or in any church fellowship at that time.

Yet the Lord, through all of our efforts to exalt and glorify me in my musical career rather than Him in a ministry to which he had called me way back in 1954, would not leave or forsake me or cast me out of His kingdom. Following the financial failure of the Opera Company until after the death of my wife in 1997 losses, illnesses and sin plagued me: loss of six different houses, several businesses and jobs and all sources of income, even two failed suicide attempts. Though I believed and never ceased praying in tongues by the Holy Spirit, the Spirit could never have penetrated my unbelief to grant my petitions until He opened my eyes to see and my ears to hear sometime in 1998. Jesus showed me that I had received the miracle of the baptism in the Holy spirit that I prayed for in 1954, but had remained all those decades an infant in Christ, basking in His one touch of glory but failing to grow into maturity.

INHERITANCE & SPIRITUAL MATURITY

Without spiritual maturity there would be nothing for me to tell you and no reason for you to read this book I am not the only one to have found the Lord and abundantly to have received His favor only to allow cares of this world and spiritual immaturity to draw me back to the dead flesh man once baptized into the Lord's death. Millions have hungered to find God and received Jesus as their Lord but without the constant stream of favor that He covered me with before I believed. Other millions of believers have stagnated in immaturity, as I have. But until we receive the full power of repentance in our hearts no amount of fervent belief will sustain us for we are to walk in faith and not mere pious belief. But in faith

Jesus, as he promises, would never leave me nor forsake me though I had long forsaken Him. But He sought me out and found me and found me a congregation where I can again worship Him in spirit and in truth, a congregation that I was too disobedient to find for myself. There is, no need for you to spend 54 years the way I did as a babe in Christ standing still in your own delusion

CHAPTER 9

Lost Sheep Found

As the apostle Paul said I now can say that all my glory that God through our Lord Jesus Christ and His Holy Spirit showered on me despite my sin and failure to glorify Him for 79 years, all that glory of all those years I can now count only as dung, the detritus of the world.

> *Phillipians 3:8*
> *Yea doubtless, and I count all things but loss for the excellency of the knowledge of Christ Jesus my Lord: for whom I have suffered the loss of all things, and do count them but dung, that I may win Christ,*

Age does not bring wisdom, Wisdom must be prayed for from the Lord and He will grant it, no matter how long you have wallowed in your folly. But He also denies no wisdom to the young who have wallowed only briefly in their folly. To accelerate your development, you have only to ask in Jesus name, and each time you receive from the Lord don't relax but ask for more. The gifts that you ask for will never cease until you cease to ask. And they will resume again as soon as you ask again for more.

> *James 4:7-8*
> *Therefore, submit to God. Resist the devil and he will flee from you. [8]Draw near to God and He will draw*

near to you. Cleanse your hands, you sinners; and purify your hearts, you double-minded.

If you believe yourself unworthy to ask from the Lord in Jesus name, you are not resisting the devil, but letting him deceive you and you can't receive, because you can't ask. Satan has you securely locked down serving his kingdom of darkness unwittingly, and the longer you wait the firmer his grip on you. You are indeed not worthy nor are any of us, for it is only Christ who makes us worthy by his grace, which he will grant as soon as asked; He is the one who qualifies you, and you can't do it yourself or any otherwise earn it. What you pray and persist in praying for is yours already, no matter how long it may take to manifest in your life. Stand and persist and you will have it and your spiritual development will be accelerated from wherever it last stopped. It is only by the deception, distraction and diversion of the world, the flesh and the devil that your spiritual development can be halted.

Remain alert to discern those deceptions that will inevitably stalk you to stop you at any point that you reach. Pray right now for the gift of discernment and you can be the one to stop Satan in his tracks through the power that Jesus has bought back for you through His resurrection. Thereby you are qualified and shall be at the next step of your growth in sanctification.

1 John 4:4
You are of God, little children, and have overcome them, because He who is in you is greater than he who is in the world.

Satan when he stops you, as he does and tries to do all the time, has not nearly the power that you do in Jesus Christ. Jesus has fully qualified you to call upon His power whenever you need it in His name. You have no need to allow any level to arrest or delay your spiritual growth. Quite the contrary, you can accelerate your spiritual development by thanking Jesus for what you prayed for in faith believing before you see it manifested. Thanks in advance for what you don't yet see seals the certainty of its manifestation, and whenever that comes will be in time for any difficulty, emergency or burden for which you supplicate Him. He is never late despite any anxiety you may suffer waiting. That anxiety is synonymous with unbelief, which we all go through in those situations. But standing, we need only to stand in faith believing, and the Lord will faithfully supply adequate faith to complete the work begun.

Faith is not something that we have to work up because it is in every case and in every quantity, great or small, a gift of God's grace, and a free gift from the resurrected Jesus, whose love casts out all fear. No fear or anxiety can help Jesus accomplish it; it can only hinder you from receiving, if you cling to it rather than thanking Him. The power of thanks is beyond calculating, and the thanks need not be alone for the things that you have prayed for. It is beneficial and effective to fill a huge storage tank with fervent thanks to hold in readiness for all possible situations. In the tank from Christ are all the qualifications that you will ever need.

The Lord is not yet finished blessing you with that storage tank of thanks, because you can fill yet others with praise, with prayer, with service, with offerings and other treasures laid up in heaven. Most of us understand prayer and that we always need more of it, though we are not yet filling up that tank. With the cares of this world and the demands on our time, the service tank is the one we most neglect to fill, and when we do fill it we are easily deceived to think that we have done something and start to break our arms patting ourselves on the back, not acknowledging that those good works are His and that we only walk in them.

Christianity always needs bigger tanks and increased funds for them to hold, because the misery in this fallen world leaves millions of people destitute in poverty, homeless, hungry, orphaned, enslaved, prostituted and hopeless. Unfortunately, Satan is the greatest there are always a few like that, led astray by the devil, but precious defender of the status quo; he likes it that way, and he succeeds quite effortlessly by convincing most parishioners that their pastors only ask for money to enrich themselves in $1,000 suits, $90,000 cars and $1,000,000 mansions. Yes few. Satan prefers anyway to mislead the multitudes instead and plant greed and distrust in their hearts.

The truth, however, is that God really owns it all and that by keeping that funding tank only half full with our tithes and offerings we could eliminate all of the worlds staggering woes in short order. That is, only a worldly assessment which will never be realized on a macro scale by mortal man. Only Jesus will accomplish that when He comes to reign on earth. But on a micro scale, husbanding the Lord's money that we consider to be our own according to the clear guidance that God has given in His word, even defying the secular laws of mathematics, the Lord can and does provide all our needs with overflow when we ask Him. He cannot do it, though, unless we seek revelation of His Word concerning our relationship with money. It is not by praying to the Lord for His provision that you gain understanding of how to escape from the worship of Mammon (money), but by revelation. Only by my testimony can I give you an explanation of how that revelation manifested in my life. I cannot impart to you that revelation; only God can by His Holy Spirit.

For the entire length of my true marriage in 1964 until 1997 when my wife died, although I knew full well that I should be paying tithe, I failed to do so, excusing myself by the fact that I fancied the pressures of the world, the flesh and the devil to be insurmountable. While being blessed and united in one flesh with the wonderful wife that God provided for me, and still clinging, though distractedly, to the precious gift and miracle of speaking and praying in tongues that I had so fervently sought and received in 1954. I drifted away from my former relentless search for holiness. I am certain that you know what I am talking about, because there is not one believer who has not similarly fallen away, short of denying God but certainly not in the center of God's perfect will.

When the Lord led me back to Himself, refusing to leave or forsake me, I started tithing regularly, despite the fact that my income had been cut by more than half. I started performing this as some kind of religious duty imposed on me by the Law of Moses. Gradually, however, the Lord began continually to pour out upon me solutions to my debt problems and enable me to budget and wipe out all my debts. Those were the material blessings, but the Lord had far more for me when he began to flood me with the consequent spiritual blessing of joy in giving.

2 Corinthians 9:7
So, let each one give as he purposes So let each one give as he purposes in his heart, not grudgingly or of necessity; for God loves a cheerful giver. in his heart, not grudgingly or of necessity; for God loves a cheerful giver.

Since receiving that joy and revelation I have been able many times to give away considerable sums and even my last widower's mite and never run short. I write this only to help you to see the way to fill your funding tank to overflowing. This very difficult thing to overcome, which is impossible without Christ's doing it within you, will accelerate your spiritual development toward sanctification, glorification and holiness at warp speed and qualify you for more abundant inheritance. No child and no adult or octogenarian, need ever heed the lies of the devil and get stuck at any stage of spiritual development when we lean for all of it upon our Lord Jesus Christ.

Although the funding tank in your heart is one of the most difficult to keep filled as you lay up your treasures in heaven by the leading of the Holy Spirit. The most important and difficult tank to keep filled and laid up in heaven is your love tank, and it must always be overflowing, never half full and never merely human natural affection for what and whom we like for a while and can change our minds about. The Love with which we must fill that tank is the unconditional love of Jesus Christ by which we reach out impassioned to the most despicable creatures on earth as vessels to extend the all-encompassing embrace of God's love.

CHAPTER 10
Walking

The incomprehensible to the carnal man as well as the carnal part remaining in the soul of the believer that has not died to the flesh or been killed off here are many words in both of God's eternal covenants that are yet. "Walk" is one of those words. We know that the apostles walked with Jesus for three years and then walked away from him hanging on the cross. Two of them walked with Him again on the road to Emmaus. One of them walked to the high priest and the Sanhedrin, then to a garden, and, when he changed his mind walked back again and then took a last walk to a field called Aceldama. The one who loved Jesus walked with His mother to the foot of the cross.

When I ask, "Where have you walked?" after mentioning these famous walks, the question begins to take on greater meaning of a different kind and a bit deeper. But we have not yet plumbed the depths of that word until we contemplate two of its most significant usages that compete with each other: to walk in the flesh and to walk in the spirit.

There is not very much substance to walking in the flesh, which consists of a little more than putting one foot in front of another, but not much more. Your flesh is your mortal body, which will die soon and prevent you from doing any more walking and you don't have very much walking of that kind left to do. If you imagine that that will give your feet a pleasant rest, please think again, because you will have arrived at your destination where there is no more walking out. As your feet burn for eternity you will never again find relief for them.

Yet we are told to walk, but to walk in the Spirit and not in the flesh. What does that mean? What's the difference? How do we do it? Can we actually do it? We do it by walking with different feet that never tire, no matter how long and how far we go, because those feet are the pedal extremities of a complete glorified and eternal body that we receive by walking in the Spirit, even when our feet hurt. The glorious and amazing thing is that when your physical feet really hurt in the flesh they can be completely relieved by walking in the Spirit. They along with every part of the flesh can be healed from any affliction, because our Lord Jesus Christ 'by his stripes' took away not only all our afflictions but also all our sin on the cross, and He heals it all when we walk not only in the Spirit, but walk also in faith believing

> *Galatians 5:16-21*
> *I say then: Walk in the Spirit, and you shall not fulfill the lust of the flesh.*
> *[17]For the flesh lusts against the Spirit, and the Spirit against the flesh; and these are contrary to one another, so that you do not do the things that you wish. [18]But if you are led by the Spirit, you are not under the law. [19]Now the works of the flesh are evident, which are: adultery, fornication, uncleanness, lewdness, [20]idolatry, sorcery, hatred, contentions, jealousies, outbursts of wrath, selfish ambitions, dissensions, heresies, [21]envy, murders, drunkenness, revelries, and the like; of which I tell you beforehand, just as I also told you in time past,*

that those who practice such things will not inherit the kingdom of God.

The walk to the kingdom of darkness is effortless and not tiring. You're already there if you choose to continue walking toward it. Your walk will not be as pleasant as you might think, for the road that you walk is paved with all pain,

Romans 1:29-31
being filled with all unrighteousness, sexual immorality, wickedness, covetousness, maliciousness; full of envy, murder, strife, deceit, evil-mindedness; they are whisperers, 30backbiters, haters of God, violent, proud, boasters, inventors of evil things, disobedient to parents, 31undiscerning, untrustworthy, unloving, unforgiving, unmerciful; 32who, knowing the righteous judgment of God, that those who practice such things are deserving of death, not only do the same but also approve of those who practice them.

Getting us to deny doing any of these things and vindicate ourselves is one of the favorite tricks of Satan, but self vindication is always the wrong way to walk.

Romans 3:23-24
for all have sinned and fall short of the glory of God, 24being justified freely by His grace through the redemption that is in Christ Jesus,

Heaven is universally recognized as a glorious and blissful place to go after death, provided it exists. Countless ways to reach heaven have been conceived of and described in detail by many 'holy' men, gurus, wise men, philosophers and scholars with elaborate doctrines, but which way must one walk to get there? Is there more than one way? Can I take my choice of which way to walk or walk a number of them simultaneously?

> *John 14:5-6*
> *Thomas said to Him, "Lord, we do not know where You are going, and how can we know the way?"*
> *⁶Jesus said to him, "I am the way, the truth, and the life. No one comes to the Father except through Me.*

> *John10:7-10*
> *Then Jesus said to them again, "Most assuredly, I say to you, I am the door of the sheep. ⁸All who ever came before Me are thieves and robbers, but the sheep did not hear them. ⁹I am the door. If anyone enters by Me, he will be saved, and will go in and out and find pasture. ¹⁰The thief does not come except to steal, and to kill, and to destroy. I have come that they may have life, and that they may have it more abundantly.*

As we walk in the Spirit we are taught and helped by the Holy Spirit to walk everywhere dispensing the overflowing, unconditional love of God in which we are to walk, beacons of his light and glory, not our own.

> *Ephesians 5:1-2*
> *Therefore, be imitators of God as dear children. ²And walk in love, as Christ also has loved us and given Himself for us, an offering and a sacrifice to God for a sweet-smelling aroma.*

1 Corinthians 13:4

Love suffers long and is kind; love does not envy; love does not parade itself, is not puffed up; [5]does not behave rudely, does not seek its own, is not provoked, thinks no evil; [6]does not rejoice in iniquity, but rejoices in the truth; [7]bears all things, believes all things, hopes all things, endures all things.

CHAPTER 11
Gifts

The day of Pentecost questions of doctrine have split Jesus Christ's church into fragments that He prayed to His Father to prevent, though He knew throughout the last two centuries with origins going back as far as it was to come. There is no possibility that His Prayer will be denied, but in His mercy, patience and long suffering He has delayed His imminent return to let us join Him in one accord in His Prayer for unity before time runs out and the coming wrath can no longer be held back.

John 17:20-26
I do not pray for these alone, but also for those who will believe in Me through their word; ²¹that they all may be one, as You, Father, are in Me, and I in You; that they also may be one in Us, that the world may believe that You sent Me. ²²And the glory which You gave Me I have given them, that they may be one just as We are one: ²³I in them, and You in Me; that they may be made perfect in one, and that the world may know that You have sent Me, and have loved them as You have loved Me.
²⁴"Father, I desire that they also whom You gave Me may be with Me where I am, that they may behold My glory which You have given Me; for You loved Me before the foundation of the world. ²⁵O righteous Father! The world has not known You, but I have known You;

and these have known that You sent Me. [26] *And I have declared to them Your name, and will declare it, that the love with which You loved Me may be in them, and I in them."*

Jesus is already providing all living, as well as those who believe on Him and His Father who sent Him, with every qualification needed to spend eternity with Him in His kingdom. He provides to us all that we could never provide. But, though we fall short of the glory of God, He has given gifts to men.

> *Ephesians 4:8*
> *Therefore, He says: "When He ascended on high, He led captivity captive, and gave gifts to men."*

> *John 3:27*
> *John answered and said, "A man can receive nothing unless it has been given to him from heaven.*

This is a glorious scriptural revelation from John the Baptist, which is part of the reason why Jesus honored him so highly, for it reveals the fact that all things that men have are gifts from God. But shortly after Jesus ascended to His Father He sent special gifts through the Holy Spirit according to the prophet Joel.

> *Joel 2:*
> *"And it shall come to pass afterward That I will pour out My Spirit on all flesh; Your sons and your daughters shall prophesy, your old men shall dream dreams, your young men shall see visions.*
> [29] *And also on My menservants and on My maidservants I will pour out My Spirit in those days.*

30 "And I will show wonders in the heavens and in the earth: Blood and fire and pillars of smoke
31The sun shall be turned into darkness, And the moon into blood, Before the coming of the great and awesome day of the LORD.
32And it shall come to pass That whoever calls on the name of the LORD Shall be saved. For in Mount Zion and in Jerusalem there shall be deliverance, As the LORD has said, Among the remnant whom the LORD calls.

At Pentecost after the Lord's ascension these gifts were poured out upon the 120 disciples gathered together in the upper room in Jerusalem, tarrying as Jesus had commanded, awaiting the baptism in the Holy Spirit to empower those few to preach the gospel to all the world.

Mark 16:17
And these signs will follow those who believe: In My name they will cast out demons; they will speak with new tongues; 18they will take up serpents; and if they drink anything deadly, it will by no means hurt them; they will lay hands on the sick, and they will recover."

Not long after these events that occurred as prophesied the thirteenth apostle, called and appointed later than the others by Jesus Christ Himself, named Saul of Tarsus, renamed Paul, revealed the use of some of these special gifts to be received and imparted by and to believers. When all authority was confiscated from common men by a Papacy in the western church and by Metropolitans in the Orthodox church usurping all power to be exercised by a soon corrupted priesthood, all these gifts along with the reading of the scriptures by laymen were gradually banned from the church only to become a major point of contention in the reformation. As we approach nearly the last chance of salvation before Jesus' coming not men's wisdom but the Lord Himself is revealing all His gifts to mankind and bringing about the fulfillment of His prayer to the Father.

> *1 Corinthians 12:4-11*
> *There are diversities of gifts, but the same Spirit. ⁵There are differences of ministries, but the same Lord. ⁶And there are diversities of activities, but it is the same God who works all in all. ⁷But the manifestation of the Spirit is given to each one for the profit of all: ⁸for to one is given the word of wisdom through the Spirit, to another the word of knowledge through the same Spirit, ⁹to another faith by the same Spirit, to another gifts of healings by the same Spirit, ¹⁰to another the working of miracles, to another prophecy, to another discerning of spirits, to another different kinds of tongues, to another the interpretation of tongues. ¹¹But one and the same Spirit works all these things, distributing to each one individually as He wills.*

In this scripture however, the Holy Spirit is not finished talking with the apostle, nor with us. In the many manifestations of these gifts throughout history, but more particularly in the last century, preachers and evangelists have made mistakes and acted according to their misinterpretations of chapter 12 without heeding all of what Paul had to say in chapters 13 and 14. Though these men were clearly in the will of God and serving His purposes in their revivals and outpourings of the Holy

Spirit, they had not yet manifested the full council of God Consequently the most prominent denominations began rejecting, editing and revising Scripture, allegedly to make it more conformable to the 'modern era' and do away with all the blood of Christ, which seems so indelicate to sensitive ladies in the congregation; and certainly God would never approve of there being a hell.

In chapter 22:18-19 of the Apocalypse or Revelation of John the consequence of any such alteration is clearly articulated by the Holy Spirit.

> [18]*For I testify to everyone who hears the words of the prophecy of this book: If anyone adds to these things, God will add to him the plagues that are written in this book;* [19]*and if anyone takes away from the words of the book of this prophecy, God shall take away his part from the Book of Life, from the holy city, and from the things which are written in this book.*

As the end of this dispensation comes closer The Lord has purposed to reveal a more complete understanding of all gifts and of His special gifts throughout the body of Christ across all denominational and cultural lines.

> *1 Corinthians 14:25-39*
> *How is it then, brethren? Whenever you come together, each of you has a psalm, has a teaching, has a tongue, has a revelation, has an interpretation. Let all things be done for edification.* [27]*If anyone speaks in a tongue, let there be two or at the most three, each in turn, and let one interpret.* [28]*But if there is no interpreter, let him keep silent in church, and let him speak to himself and to God.* [29]*Let two or three prophets speak, and let the*

others judge. ³⁰But if anything is revealed to another who sits by, let the first keep silent. ³¹For you can all prophesy one by one, that all may learn and all may be encouraged. ³²And the spirits of the prophets are subject to the prophets. ³³For God is not the author of confusion but of peace, as in all the churches of the saints.

³⁴Let your women keep silent in the churches, for they are not permitted to speak; but they are to be submissive, as the law also says. ³⁵And if they want to learn something, let them ask their own husbands at home; for it is shameful for women to speak in church.

³⁹Or did the word of God come originally from you? Or was it you only that it reached? ³⁷If anyone thinks himself to be a prophet or spiritual, let him acknowledge that the things which I write to you are the commandments of the Lord. ³⁸But if anyone is ignorant, let him be ignorant. Therefore, brethren, desire earnestly to prophesy, and do not forbid to speak with tongues. ⁴⁰Let all things be done decently and in order.

Confusion and disorder in the church, the body of Christ, are not conducive to unity in His body, the unity that He prayed for in John 17. And God will settle for nothing less than unity. Local and even widespread revivals that fail to be poured out on all flesh reflect the obstacles that disunity prevailing in the churches and their faulty hermeneutics (varying interpretations). Where disharmony and strife persist, the Holy Spirit is hindered.

Because giving thanks to God for His gifts is essential to cause them to blossom into full bloom, we should distinguish which gifts are which and start with those that all men receive at birth and possess until the death of the physical body, whether spiritually redeemed or not. Another category of gifts is those that we receive at salvation when we are justified and reborn as new creatures in Christ; these must be clearly distinguished from the special gifts of the Holy Spirit that we receive with the baptism of the Holy Spirit.

1. At birth we receive the breath of life, a mortal body in which to dwell for a short time. The body may be perfect, strong and beautiful, or it may be ill, weak or deformed. Whatever it is its all that we have and we need to be thankful for it, and through thanks we can accomplish miraculous things through Christ like Nick Vujicic, born without arms or legs, now preaching Christ traveling around the world. Whether born into a loving, wealthy family or the most wretched circumstances we need to be thankful for whatever it is, and for whatever nurture and care we receive.

2. Upon believing in our hearts and confessing with our mouths, speaking that Jesus Christ is the living resurrected Son of God and inviting Him into our hearts we receive not only eternal life, a new birth as a totally new spiritual creature with Jesus Himself living inside us along with His Holy Spirit, but also justification before God and forgiveness of all our sin. This is the most glorious gift of His Grace. As believers we also receive a job assignment which we must undertake and fulfill, if we hope to receive the better parts of our inheritance.

Mark 16:15-16
And He said to them, "Go into all the world and preach the gospel to every creature. ¹⁶He who believes and is

baptized will be saved; but he who does not believe will
be condemned.

Almost every church member, though fully aware of these two verses of Mark's gospel but avoids or edits out the next two

Mark 16:17-18
And these signs will follow those who believe: In My
name they will cast out demons; they will speak with
new tongues; ¹⁸they will take up serpents; and if they
drink anything deadly, it will by no means hurt them;
they will lay hands on the sick, and they will recover."

These are the ordinary signs that every believer should be manifesting in every church and believing family. But where are they? These signs are distributed to every believer and available for all believers to call upon at all times, not only anointed pastors, teachers and prophets. Though doubters vigorously insist that such things were only for the 'early church', none has ever provided a scriptural confirmation of that foolish notion.

3. The nine special gifts of the Holy Spirit described in Paul's first letter to the Corinthians can and should be sought by all believers, but are distributed only as the Holy Spirit wills, whereas the distribution of signs in Mark 16:17–18 are given and accessible to all believers. That does not mean that all churches must gather cobras and rattle snakes to test the faith of their parishioners nor distribute cyanide and strychnine for that purpose. It does mean though that a believer is safe in snake-infested areas and suffers no harm

83

from accidentally ingested poisons when in faith believing. However, casting out demons, speaking in new tongues and laying hands on the sick in Jesus' name are not reserved only for special occasions or persons, they are the province of all believers as signs for unbelievers.

The nine gifts of the Holy Spirit differ from the signs that follow believers in that they must be sought and are for use in ministry however the Holy Spirit distributes them.

a. The word of wisdom is given by the Holy Spirit for edification of the receiver or another person
b. A word of knowledge is given by the Spirit to inform the receivers
c. A special extra measure of faith is given by the same Spirit
d. To another the Spirit gives a special gift and ministry of healing, greater than the sign to which all believers have access.
e. To others the Spirits gives the power to perform miracles.
f. Yet others receive from the Spirit the gift of prophesy for informing, building up and edifying the church.
g. To others is given the gift of discerning of spirits, whether they be of God or of the devil.
h. Another special gift of the Holy Spirit is the speaking of various unknown tongues of men and angels, greater than the sign that all believers display.
i. The Spirit also gives to some the gift of interpreting other tongues, whose interpretations amount to prophecy.

The whole body of Christ desperately needs in these last days to receive and call upon all of these signs and gifts while there is yet time. It is no insurmountable task to receive these gifts; the Holy Spirit qualifies every one who asks in faith believing and in obedience to the Word of God, and an additional gift with which the Lord rewards obedience is more obedience.

CHAPTER 12
Grace

A mong all the words in the Bible perhaps 'grace' is the one most easily diminished and tossed off the tongue of Christians in ignorance of its meaning, since the word and its derivatives are widely used in secular society with completely different meaning. Believers quite easily and often use the word in its secular sense without pausing to reflect on its true and sacred sense. In that true sense grace encompasses all things in the universe. Jesus Christ is the creator of the universe and the glory of God as well as being the grace by which He created all things and gives all things to mankind. By faith through grace we are saved

We probably understand better the Latin word 'gratis' from which 'grace' is derived. We know that 'gratis' refers to something that we can get for free, without cost, but we have trouble retaining in our consciousness the fact that 'grace' in the spiritual context means the same thing: Things that we have received and can receive free and only without cost; we have not paid for them and can never have them at all by paying any price, because they are only obtainable by grace. And Jesus is the only manifestation and substance of that grace. That, I am certain, bears little resemblance to the grace of a gracious host or hostess or the gracious movements of a dancer.

What we have all received by grace is the breath of life, the shape and functions of our bodies, our eye color, our hair color our skin color, our brains, our minds, our talents or natural gifts, etc. What is available to us through grace is everything else. How you do it I don't know, but we Christians along with all the rest of humanity let it slip our minds that Jesus by his grace has already bought for us all things in creation that we desire and struggle to acquire by paying the price of our efforts to get them without His grace.

First, we try to crash our way into heaven by some kind of good works or religious observance that inevitably leaves us empty. Only when we cease trying to break in and turn to His grace are we able to receive by grace eternal life. And it is only by grace that we reached the point of asking because God loved us first. We have access to all of His promises, His signs and wonders by grace and we receive them by grace. And by grace we pass from death to life in faith. By grace we receive answer to prayer, healing, provision, health, strength, revelation, deliverance from addiction and sexual immorality, protection for our families on earth, and inheritance in heaven.

By God's grace you already have both all that you have asked for and all that you have not yet asked for; it is all there for you to receive as soon as you ask for it. And it is Jesus who has qualified all who believe in His death and resurrection and that His Father sent Him, He has qualified all through his grace to inherit all things in heaven, all for which you have faith. All faith required is already a gift of His grace within you that you merely have to engage and persistently continue engaging at each step of your spiritual growth. And each level of growth can be either a terminal destination or a new starting point to the next higher level according to your choice. If you chose not to go higher, God honors that choice and limits your inheritance, not as punishment, but according to your choice. In any and all cases it is by the grace of God that you have arrived at the level where you stopped; Whatever level of faith you have exercised has confirmed by grace your eternal life in heaven that no power on earth can take away from you. But there is no level of grace that exhausts grace, for God's grace is infinite beyond the confines of time and space, the universe and this creation.

There is never a point where you need to stop or slow down in God's grace. The Holy Spirit by God's grace is always with you and available to show and teach you the way all the way to infinity and comfort you along the way through Jesus Christ, who is Himself both love and grace.

> *John 1:16-17*
> *And of His fullness we have all received, and grace for grace. [17]For the law was given through Moses, but grace and truth came through Jesus Christ.*

The process of receiving grace for grace described by John the Baptist is parallel to the similar process of growing from faith to faith

> *Romans 1:16-17*
> *For I am not ashamed of the gospel of Christ, for it is the power of God to salvation for everyone who believes, for the Jew first and also for the Greek. [17]For in it the righteousness of God is revealed from faith to faith; as it is written, "The just shall live by faith."*

CHAPTER 13
Sanctification

You will understand little, profit little and advance little by reading this chapter unless you have first secured your eternal salvation and justification before God by believing in your heart that Jesus Christ is the living Son of God who died on the cross at Calvary taking away upon Himself all the sin, sickness and disease of the world; and that he rose again from the grave after three days to ascend alive to His Father who sent Him and to make intercession for us until His coming to rule and reign forever. Also, you should by now have made public declaration of your belief at this point you need not understand all of that; you need only to believe and declare that you believe and believe that you have thereby received eternal life whether you understand it yet or not.

All of that is the greatest miracle in creation but it is only a launching pad from which you can soar into heavenly realms immediately or remain standing still in awe for weeks, months, years or decades according to your precious gift of choice; as an infant in Christ just barely across the threshold of heaven gaining little if any spiritual inheritance. Since the limitless love of God for you is so great his will and purpose for you is that you should enter into a process of sanctification that will lead you to glorification and eventually to holiness; that you joy might be complete.

John 15:9-11

"As the Father loved Me, I also have loved you; abide in My love. ¹⁰If you keep My commandments, you will abide in My love, just as I have kept My Father's commandments and abide in His love. These things I have spoken to you, that My joy may remain in you, and that your joy may be full.

These things Jesus uttered to His disciples after His resurrection and before His ascension to His Father and before they had received the baptism in the Holy Spirit. Only at that time, after walking for three years with the incarnate son of God did the disciples become the first to receive the salvation and redemption that you have received by believing in your heart.

John 20:21-22

So, Jesus said to them again, "Peace to you! As the Father has sent Me, I also send you." ²²And when He had said this, He breathed on them, and said to them, "Receive the Holy Spirit.

When you believed you received the Holy Spirit as they did, but they were told to wait in Jerusalem until the comforter came to them so that they might receive power through the baptism in the Holy Spirit.

John 16:7-15

⁷Nevertheless, I tell you the truth. It is to your advantage that I go away; for if I do not go away, the Helper will not come to you; but if I depart, I will send Him to you. ⁸And when He has come, He will convict the world of sin, and of righteousness, and of judgment: ⁹of sin, because they do not believe in Me; ¹⁰of righteousness,

because I go to My Father and you see Me no more;
¹¹of judgment, because the ruler of this world is judged.
¹² "I still have many things to say to you, but you cannot
bear them now. ¹³However, when He, the Spirit of
truth, has come, He will guide you into all truth; for
He will not speak on His own authority, but whatever
He hears He will speak; and He will tell you things to
come. ¹⁴He will glorify Me, for He will take of what is
Mine and declare it to you. ¹⁵All things that the Father
has are Mine. Therefore, I said that He will take of
Mine and declare it to you.

Luke 24:49
Behold, I send the Promise of My Father upon you; but
tarry in the city of Jerusalem until you are endued with
power from on high."

And they did wait and they did receive power, the
power by which those eleven men and a twelfth, appointed
to replace Judas the betrayer, changed forever the course of
history on earth. That power has never diminished and it
will yet soon complete the task, the mission, for which it
was sent. Satan, who once had you fully qualified for his
kingdom and his eternal lake of fire, has been engaged in
the church of God, the body of Christ, to persuade believers
to think that that power has been withdrawn along with
speaking in tongues, gifts of the Spirit, the blood of Jesus
and miracles; he says that those things were for the so called
'early church', they have no place in his church. But all the
denominations into which the devil has managed to split
the Church will in these last days come together in unity,
as Jesus has prayed to the Father to exercise that power and
every knee shall bow.

Phillipians 2:9-11
Therefore, God also has highly exalted Him and given Him the name which is above every name, ¹⁰that at the name of Jesus every knee should bow, of those in heaven, and of those on earth, and of those under the earth, ¹¹and that every tongue should confess that Jesus Christ is Lord, to the glory of God the Father.

John 6:63
It is the Spirit who gives life; the flesh profits nothing. The words that I speak to you are spirit, and they are life.

1 Thesalonians 5:16-18
Rejoice always, ¹⁷pray without ceasing, ¹⁸in everything give thanks; for this is the will of God in Christ Jesus for you. ¹⁹Do not quench the Spirit. ²⁰Do not despise prophecies. ²¹Test all things; hold fast what is good. ²²Abstain from every form of evil.

In setting out determinedly to manifest our sanctification we must have all powers and forces in place, at the ready to confront any attack of the enemy, who, though defeated at the cross, remains wiley, deceptive and powerful. In these scriptures we find our defensive weapons and, in many others, yet to be cited. These are not, however, any kind of truncated but adequate Bible. No such thing exists, and the seeker of sanctification needs to have command of the full council of God in both the New and the Old Testaments.

2 Timothy 3:16
All Scripture is given by inspiration of God, and is profitable for doctrine, for reproof, for correction, for instruction in righteousness, ¹⁷that the man of God may be complete, thoroughly equipped for every good work.

2 Peter 1:19-20
And so, we have the prophetic word confirmed, which
you do well to heed as a light that shines in a dark
place, until the day dawns and the morning star rises
in your hearts; ²⁰knowing this first, that no prophecy of
Scripture is of any private interpretation, ²¹for prophecy
never came by the will of man, but holy men of God
spoke as they were moved by the Holy Spirit.

As the seeker delves deeper into the mysteries of God
he must be wary of the wiles of the devil who has often
led the faithful astray to imagine that what they receive
from the Lord in prophecy, words of wisdom, words of
knowledge, dreams and visions are revelations co-equal
with or superseding the canonical scriptures. They are
not! Such are the 'revelations' that are the stock in trade
of countless false prophets and anti-christs that infest the
churches, the world and the last days. And add to that.

Galatians 6:20-21
¹⁷I say then: Walk in the Spirit, and you shall not
fulfill the lust of the flesh.
For the flesh lusts against the Spirit, and the Spirit
against the flesh; and these are contrary to one
another, so that you do not do the things that you
wish. ¹⁸But if you are led by the Spirit, you are
not under the law.
¹⁹Now the works of the flesh are evident, which
are: adultery, fornication, uncleanness, lewdness,
²⁰idolatry, sorcery, hatred, contentions, jealousies,
outbursts of wrath, selfish ambitions, dissensions,
heresies, ²¹envy, murders, drunkenness, revelries,
and the like; of which I tell you beforehand, just
as I also told *you* in time past, that those who

practice such things will not inherit the kingdom of God. Although sorcery is perhaps not the most prominent thing in the list of evils, its many facets make it the most destructive and diabolic. Those facets include Deceptive arts and charms practiced by designing men, and classed with magic, divination, witchcraft, and necromancy, there is, however, in the same chapter a list of the fruits of the Spirit by which one can measure his progress in sanctification.

Galatians 5:22
*But the fruit of the Spirit is love, joy, peace, longsuffering, kindness, goodness, faithfulness, *[23]*gentleness, self-control. Against such there is no law. *[24]*And those who are Christ's have crucified the flesh with its passions and desires. *[25]*If we live in the Spirit, let us also walk in the Spirit.*

Although it might seem that there are more qualifications to fulfill in Christ than there are in the secular world, which demands schooling, good grade point averages, degrees, graduate degrees, internships, residencies, experience, clean criminal and driving records, proper insurance coverage, clean banking records, etc., Jesus has paid the price for all of your sanctification and qualifies you at each step of the way that you chose to follow, and his timing for gifts, sanctification and blessings is always now, as opposed to the world's demands for decades of drudgery to achieve anything; and what one has achieved is soon gone and forgotten.*.God's sanctification is forever.

CHAPTER 14
Glorification

E nough holiness to be permitted while still on earth to go briefly to heaven and to see the glory of God, and to return to earth and report in throughout history there have always been a few who have achieved some always inadequate way what they have experienced and how their experience conforms with revelation in the Word of God. Just as you probably do, I deeply regret that I have not been one of those people.

I know of none who can draw any satisfactory analogies to our glorification or their own. Words fail them to describe the glory of God or his majesty. The only and probably best glimpse that most of us are likely to see of His mysteries while still on earth and walking in the flesh is to be found in the scriptures as the Holy Spirit reveals. That is how those who have seen received their revelation

All of us who have believed and been redeemed by the blood of Jesus and have neither had revealed a vision of heaven or the glory of *God, nor received revelation of what our glorification will be can take consolation in the truth that Jesus spoke to Thomas who required so much evidence from the risen Lord standing before his eyes and insisting that he probe His wounds with his hands.*

Though after touching the wounds on Jesus' hands and feet and thrusting his hand in his side Thomas finally confessed, "My Lord and my God, Jesus rebuked him and revealed our consolation.

> *John 20:29*
> *Now Thomas, called the Twin, one of the twelve, was not with them when Jesus came. ²⁵The other disciples therefore said to him, "We have seen the Lord."*
> *So, he said to them, "Unless I see in His hands the print of the nails and put my finger into the print of the nails, and put my hand into His side, I will not believe."*
> *²⁶And after eight days His disciples were again inside, and Thomas with them. Jesus came, the doors being shut, and stood in the midst, and said, "Peace to you!"*
> *²⁷Then He said to Thomas, "Reach your finger here, and look at My hands; and reach your hand here and put it into My side. Do not be unbelieving but believing."*
> *²⁸And Thomas answered and said to Him, "My Lord and my God!"*
> *²⁹Jesus said to him, "Thomas, because you have seen Me, you have believed. Blessed are those who have not seen and yet have believed."*

CHAPTER 15
Everlasting Covenants

Each of God's covenants described below is an everlasting covenant with man, into whom God breathed eternal life and to whom He also gave dominion over the earth. God never annulled His first covenant when man breached it, and in His ultimate purpose He will yet fulfill it. Rather than annul that covenant with Adam He made another everlasting covenant with him with the promise of a redeemer.

For several thousand years afterward, mankind manifested only evil and God, grieved in his heart, decided to obliterate all life from the earth in a universal flood, saving only Noah, whom He found righteous, and his family. After the universal flood God sent Noah forth from the ark with the animals he had preserved with a command to be fruitful and multiply and replenish the earth. And God made a covenant with Noah never again to destroy the earth by flood.

The generations and nations that followed Noah fell right back into unlimited wickedness and God called for himself a man who would both believe in Him and obey His commands in order to establish a chosen nation to bless all the nations of the world. And He made His Promises to Abram, who by faith and obedience became that man, also becoming Abraham. The promises to Abraham in the

Abrahamic covenant were better, but 400 years of slavery that his descendants were predicted to endure came to pass and required a still better covenant.

As prophesied, Moses was sent to deliver Gods chosen people out of the hand of Pharaoh of Egypt, deliver to them another covenant, the law of God, and take them into the Promised Land. The chosen people, however, were rebellious and full of unbelief.

Forty years later when Israel's surviving children had passed over to possess the land they too were rebellious and demanded that God give them a king like the other nations. That king was disobedient and a disaster for Israel, and the Lord had Samuel anoint a new king after His own heart and made with him an everlasting covenant promising that the redeemer king would sit on his throne and reign forever.

The new and final Covenant is the culmination and fulfillment of all the previous covenants and Jesus Christ is the only savior, the way, the truth and the life, waited for millennia.

I. The Edenic Covenant

Man is charged with responsibility for propagating the race, subduing the earth, exercising dominion over the animals, caring for the garden in Eden, and refraining from eating of the tree of the knowledge of good and evil.

"And God blessed them, and God said to them, 'Be fruitful and multiply, and fill the earth and subdue it; and have dominion over the fish of the sea and over the birds of the air and over every living thing that moves upon the earth.' And God said, 'Behold, I have given you every plant yielding seed which is upon the face

of all the earth, and every tree with seed in its fruit; you shall have them for food. And to every beast of the earth, and to every bird of the air, and to everything that creeps on the earth, everything that has the breath of life, I have given every green plant for food.' And it was so." (Gen. 1:28-30)

"And the LORD God commanded the man, saying, 'You may freely eat of every tree of the garden; but of the tree of the knowledge of good and evil you shall not eat, for in the day that you eat of it you shall die.'" (Gen. 2:16, 17)

II. The Adamic Covenant

See Genesis 3. Consequences of man's fall necessitated a changed relationship between man and God including the following elements: (1) A curse on the serpent:
Gen 3:14, Rom. 16:20, 2 Cor. 11:3,14, Rev. 12:9. (2) The first promise of a redeemer (the proto-evangelium). Messiah would come in the line of Seth, Noah. Shem, Abraham, Isaac, Jacob, Judah and David. (3) A changed state of woman including bondage and subservience to man's headship, and suffering and pain in motherhood. (4) Loss of the garden in Eden as a dwelling place and light occupation changed to heavy burden of work because of a cursed earth. (5) Inevitable sorrow and disappointment in life. (6) Shortened life span and tragedy of death.

III. The Noahdic Covenant

This unconditional covenant with Noah (which affects all mankind) establishes principles for all government and includes the following: (1) Sanctity of all human life established. Man responsible to protect life, even to capital punishment. (2) A Promise that another universal flood will not occur and the ground will not be cursed further. (3) Man's relationship to the animals and to nature is confirmed (Gen. 8:22, 9:2). (4) Man, presumably a vegetarian before the flood, is now allowed to eat meat. (5) Special characteristics are assigned to the three sons of Noah, Shem, Ham, and Japheth.

"And when the LORD smelled the pleasing odor, the LORD said in his heart, 'I will never again curse the ground because of man, for the imagination of man's heart is evil from his youth; neither will I ever again destroy every living creature as I have done. While the earth remains, seed time and harvest, cold and heat, summer and winter, day and night, shall not cease.' And God blessed Noah and his sons, and said to them, 'Be fruitful and multiply, and fill the earth. The fear of you and the dread of you shall be upon every beast of the earth, and upon every bird of the air, upon everything that creeps on the ground and all the fish of the sea; into your hand they are delivered. Every moving thing that lives shall be food for you; and as I gave you the green plants, I give you everything. Only you shall not eat flesh with its life, that is, its blood. For your lifeblood I will surely require a reckoning; of every beast I will require it and of man; of every man's brother I will require the life of man. Whoever sheds the blood of man, by man shall his blood be shed; for God made man in his own image. And you, be fruitful and multiply, bring forth abundantly on the earth and multiply in it.' "Then God said to Noah and to his sons with him, 'Behold, I establish my covenant with you and your descendants after you, and with every living creature that is with you, the birds, the cattle, and every beast of the earth with you, as many as came out of the ark. I establish my covenant with you, that never again shall all flesh be cut off by the waters of a flood,

and never again shall there be a flood to destroy the earth.' And God said, 'This is the sign of the covenant which I make between me and you and every living creature that is with you, for all future generations: I set my bow in the cloud, and it shall be a sign of the covenant between me and the earth. When I bring clouds over the earth and the bow is seen in the clouds, I will remember my covenant which is between me and you and every living creature of all flesh; and the waters shall never again become a flood to destroy all flesh. When the bow is in the clouds, I will look upon it and remember the everlasting covenant between God and every living creature of all flesh that is upon the earth.' God said to Noah, 'This is the sign of the covenant which I have established between me and all flesh that is upon the earth." (Gen. 8:21-9:17)

IV. The Abrahamic Covenant

An unconditional covenant. (1) God gave Abraham the promise of a great nation—primarily meaning Israel, but also includes great peoples in the line of Ishmael and Abraham's others sons. In all Abraham, had eight sons, six through his second wife Keturah after Sarah died, (Gen. 25:3). Two peoples descended from Abraham are named specially. They are an earthly group (Israel) "as numerous as the grains of sand on the seashore," and a heavenly group (the true church) "as numerous as the stars in the heavens." These two "family trees" form the subject of the mainstream of redemptive history in the Bible. (2) Abraham was chosen to be the father of numerous descendants, to be blessed personally, to be personally honored, to be a channel of blessing to others. (3) Those who bless Abraham are to be blessed and those who curse him will be cursed. Blessings on the nations are to come through Abraham.

⁴Reaffirmation of the promise of a Messiah was made by God to Abraham. *"Now the LORD said to Abram, 'Go from your country and your kindred and your father's house to the land that I will show you. And I will make of you a great nation, and I will bless you, and make your name great, so that you will be a blessing. I will bless those who bless you, and him who curses you I will curse; and by you all the families of the earth shall bless themselves.' So, Abram went, as the LORD had told him; and Lot went with him. Abram was seventy-five years old when he departed from Haran. And Abram took Sarai his wife, and Lot his brother's son, and all their possessions which they had gathered, and the persons that they had gotten in Haran; and they set forth to go to the land of Canaan. When they had come to the land of Canaan, Abram passed through the land to the place at Shechem, to the oak of Moreh. At that time the Canaanites were in the land. Then the LORD appeared to Abram, and said, 'To your descendants I will give this land.' So, he built there an altar to the LORD, who had appeared to him."* (Gen. 12:1-7)

"The LORD said to Abram, after Lot had separated from him, 'Lift up your eyes, and look from the place where you are, northward and southward and eastward and westward; for all the land which you see I will give to you and to your descendants for ever. I will make your descendants as the dust of the earth; so that if one can count the dust of the earth, your descendants also can be counted. Arise, walk through the length and the breadth of the land, for I will give it to you." (Gen. 13:14-17)

"After these things the word of the LORD came to Abram in a vision, 'Fear not, Abram, I am your shield; your reward shall be very great.' But Abram said, "O Lord GOD, what wilt thou give me, for I continue childless, and the heir of my house is Eliezer of Damascus?" And Abram said, 'Behold, thou hast given me no offspring; and a slave born in my house will be my heir.' And

behold, the word of the LORD came to him, 'This man shall not be your heir; your own son shall be your heir.' And he brought him outside and said, 'Look toward heaven, and number the stars, if you are able to number them.' Then he said to him, 'So shall your descendants be.' And he believed the LORD; and he reckoned it to him as righteousness. And he said to him, 'I am the LORD who brought you from Ur of the Chaldeans, to give you this land to possess.' But he said, 'O Lord GOD, how am I to know that I shall possess it?' He said to him, 'Bring me a heifer three-year-old, some she-goat three years old, a ram three years old, a turtledove, and a young pigeon.' And he brought him all these, cut them in two, and laid each half over against the other; but he did not cut the birds in two. And when birds of prey came down upon the carcasses, Abram drove them away. As the sun was going down, a deep sleep fell on Abram; and lo, a dread and great darkness fell upon him. "Then the LORD said to Abram, 'Know of a surety that your descendants will be sojourners in a land that is not theirs, and will be slaves there, and they will be oppressed for four hundred years; but I will bring judgment on the nation which they serve, and afterward they shall come out with great possessions. As for yourself, you shall go to your fathers in peace; you shall be buried in a good old age. And they shall come back here in the fourth generation; for the iniquity of the Amorites is not yet complete.' When the sun had gone down and it was dark, behold, a smoking fire pot and a flaming torch passed between these pieces. On that day the LORD made a covenant with Abram, saying, 'To your descendants I give this land, from the river of Egypt to the great river, the river Euphrates, the land of the Kenites, the Kenizzites, the Kadmonites, the Hittites, the Perizzites, the Rephaim, the Amorites, the Canaanites, the Girgashites and the Jebusites." (Gen 15:1-21)

"And the angel of the LORD called to Abraham a second time from heaven, and said, 'By myself I have sworn, says the LORD, because you have done this, and have not withheld your son, your only son, I will indeed bless you, and I will multiply your descendants as the stars of heaven and as the sand which is on the seashore. And your descendants shall possess the gate of their enemies, and by your descendants shall all the nations of the earth bless themselves, because you have obeyed my voice." (Gen. 22:15-18)

The Covenant With Abraham Is Restated And Confirmed To Isaac By The Lord

"And Isaac went to Gerar, to Abimelech king of the Philistines. And the LORD appeared to him, and said, 'Do not go down to Egypt; dwell in the land of which I shall tell you. Sojourn in this land, and I will be with you, and will bless you; for to you and to your descendants I will give all these lands, and I will fulfill the oath which I swore to Abraham your father. I will multiply your descendants as the stars of heaven, and will give to your descendants all these lands; and by your descendants all the nations of the earth shall bless themselves: because Abraham obeyed my voice and kept my charge, my commandments, my statutes, and my laws." (Gen. 26:1-5)

The Covenant With Abraham Is Restated And Confirmed To Jacob By The Lord

"Jacob left Beersheba, and went toward Haran. And he came to a certain place, and stayed there that night, because the sun had set. Taking one of the stones of the place, he put it under his head and lay down in that place to sleep. And he dreamed that there was a ladder set up on the earth, and the top of it reached to heaven; and behold, the angels of God were ascending and

descending on it! And behold, the LORD stood above it and said, 'I am the LORD, the God of Abraham your father and the God of Isaac; the land on which you lie I will give to you and to your descendants; and your descendants shall be like the dust of the earth, and you shall spread abroad to the west and to the east and to the north and to the south; and by you and your descendants shall all the families of the earth bless themselves. Behold, I am with you and will keep you wherever you go, and will bring you back to this land; for I will not leave you until I have done that of which I have spoken to you.'" (Gen. 28:10-15)

V. The Mosaic Covenant

A Conditional Covenant. Connected with the giving of the Law at Sinai, and the Levitical priesthood. The Law condemns all men.

"And Moses went up to God, and the LORD called to him out of the mountain, saying, 'Thus you shall say to the house of Jacob, and tell the people of Israel: You have seen what I did to the Egyptians, and how I bore you on eagles' wings and brought you to myself. Now therefore, if you will obey my voice and keep my covenant, you shall be my own possession among all peoples; for all the earth is mine, and you shall be to me a kingdom of priests and a holy nation. These are the words which you shall speak to the children of Israel." (Exodus 19:3-6)

The New Testament Comments On The Mosaic (Old) Covenant

"Now if the dispensation of death, carved in letters on stone, came with such splendor that the Israelites could not look at Moses' face because of its brightness, fading as this was, will not the dispensation of the Spirit be attended with greater splendor? For if there was

105

splendor in the dispensation of condemnation, the dispensation of righteousness must far exceed it in splendor." (2 Cor. 3:7-9)

"Now we know that whatever the law says it speaks to those who are under the law, so that every mouth may be stopped, and the whole world may be held accountable to God. For no human being will be justified in his sight by works of the law, since through the law comes knowledge of sin." (Rom. 3:19,20)

"For since the law has but a shadow of the good things to come instead of the true form of these realities, it can never, by the same sacrifices which are continually offered year after year, make perfect those who draw near.

Otherwise, would they not have ceased to be offered? If the worshipers had once been cleansed, they would no longer have any consciousness of sin. But in these sacrifices, there is a reminder of sin year after year. For it is impossible that the blood of bulls and goats should take away sins. Consequently, when Christ came into the world, he said, 'Sacrifices and offerings thou hast not desired, but a body hast thou prepared for me; in burnt offerings and sin offerings thou hast taken no pleasure. Then I said, 'Lo, I have come to do thy will, O God,' as it is written of me in the roll of the book.' When he said above, 'Thou hast neither desired nor taken pleasure in sacrifices and offerings and burnt offerings and sin offerings' (these are offered according to the law), then he added, 'Lo, I have come to do thy will.' He abolishes the first in order to establish the second. And by that will we have been sanctified through the offering of the body of Jesus Christ once for all." (Heb. 10:1-10)

VI. The Palestinian Covenant

This partly conditional covenant has several parts: (1) dispersion of the Jews was to be a consequence of disobedience. (2) Future repentance will be accomplished by God. (3) God will regather his scattered people and restore them to the land. (4) The people of Israel will be brought to the Lord as a nation. (5) The enemies and oppressors of Israel will be punished. (6) Future national prosperity and preeminence is guaranteed. See also Deut. 28, 29. Because of this covenant, the right of the Jews to live in the land is conditional upon their behavior.

"When all these things come upon you, the blessing and the curse, which I have set before you, and you call them to mind among all the nations where the LORD your God has driven you, and return to the LORD your God, you and your children, and obey his voice in all that I command you this day, with all your heart and with all your soul; then the LORD your God will restore your fortunes, and have compassion upon you, and he will gather you again from all the peoples where the LORD your God has scattered you. If your outcasts are in the uttermost parts of heaven, from there the LORD your God will gather you, and from there he will fetch you; and the LORD your God will bring you into the land which your fathers possessed, that you may possess it; and he will make you more prosperous and numerous than your fathers. And the LORD your God will circumcise your heart and the heart of your offspring, so that you will love the LORD your God with all your heart and with all your soul, that you may live. And the LORD your God will put all these curses upon your foes and enemies who persecuted you. And you shall again obey the voice of the LORD, and keep all his commandments which I command you this day. The LORD your God will make you abundantly prosperous in all the work of your hand, in the fruit of your body, and in the fruit of your cattle, and in the fruit of your ground; for the LORD will again take delight in prospering you, as he took delight in your fathers, if you obey the voice of the LORD your God, to keep his commandments and his statutes which are written

in this book of the law, if you turn to the LORD your God with all your heart and with all your soul.

"'For this commandment which I command you this day is not too hard for you, neither is it far off. It is not in heaven, that you should say, 'Who will go up for us to heaven, and bring it to us, that we may hear it and do it?' Neither is it beyond the sea, that you should say, 'Who will go over the sea for us, and bring it to us, that we may hear it and do it?" But the word is very near you; it is in your mouth and in your heart, so that you can do it. 'See, I have set before you this day life and good, death and evil. If you obey the commandments of the LORD your God which I command you this day, by loving the LORD your God, by walking in his ways, and by keeping his commandments and his statutes and his ordinances, then you shall live and multiply, and the LORD your God will bless you in the land which you are entering to take possession of it. But if your heart turns away, and you will not hear, but are drawn away to worship other gods and serve them, I declare to you this day, that you shall perish; you shall not live long in the land which you are going over the Jordan to enter and possess. I call heaven and earth to witness against you this day, that I have set before you life and death, blessing and curse; therefore choose life, that you and your descendants may live, loving the LORD your God, obeying his voice, and cleaving to him; for that means life to you and length of days, that you may dwell in the land which the LORD swore to your fathers, to Abraham, to Isaac, and to Jacob, to give them." (Deut. 30)

"For lo, I will command, and shake the house of Israel among all the nations as one shakes with a sieve, but no pebble shall fall upon the earth. All the sinners of my people shall die by the sword, who say, 'Evil shall not overtake or meet us.' 'In that day I will raise up the booth of David that is fallen and repair its breaches, and raise up its ruins, and rebuild it as in the days of old; that *they may possess the remnant of Edom and all the nations who are called by my name,' says the LORD who does this. 'Behold, the days are coming,' says the LORD, 'when the plowman shall overtake the reaper and the treader of grapes him who sows the seed; the mountains shall drip sweet wine, and all the hills shall flow with it. I will restore the fortunes of my people Israel, and they shall rebuild the ruined cities and inhabit them; they shall plant vineyards and drink their wine, and they shall make gardens and eat their fruit. I will plant them upon their land, and they shall never again be plucked up out of the land which I have given them,' says the LORD your God."* (Amos 9:9-15)

The New Testament Promises God Will Resume His Fulfillment Of Various Covenants With Israel

"Simeon [Peter] has related how God first visited the Gentiles, to take out of them a people for his name. And with this the words of the prophets agree, as it is written, *'After this I will return, and I will rebuild the dwelling of David, which has fallen; I will rebuild its ruins, and I will set it up, that the rest of men may seek the Lord, and all the Gentiles who are called by my name, says the Lord, who has made these things known from of old.'"* (Acts 15:14-18)

"and so, all Israel will be saved; as it is written, 'The Deliverer will come from Zion, he will banish ungodliness from Jacob'; 'and this will be my covenant with them when I take away their sins." (Rom. 11:26, 27)

The Old Testament Concurs

"In that day the Lord will extend his hand yet a second time to recover the remnant which is left of his people, from Assyria,

from Egypt, from Pathros, from Ethiopia, from Elam, from Shinar, from Hamath, and from the coastlands of the sea. He will raise an ensign for the nations, and will assemble the outcasts of Israel, and gather the dispersed of Judah from the four corners of the earth." (Isa. 11:11,12)

"Then I will gather the remnant of my flock out of all the countries where I have driven them, and I will bring them back to their fold, and they shall be fruitful and multiply. I will set shepherds over them who will care for them, and they shall fear no more, nor be dismayed, neither shall any be missing, says the LORD. 'Behold, the days are coming, says the LORD, when I will raise up for David a righteous Branch, and he shall reign as king and deal wisely, and shall execute justice and righteousness in the land. In his days Judah will be saved, and Israel will dwell securely. And this is the name by which he will be called: 'The LORD is our righteousness.' Therefore, behold, the days are coming, says the LORD, when men shall no longer say, 'As the LORD lives who brought up the people of Israel out of the land of Egypt,' but 'As the LORD lives who brought up and led the descendants of the house of Israel out of the north country and out of all the countries where he had driven them.' Then they shall dwell in their own land." (Jer. 23:3-8)

". . . Thus says the Lord GOD: Behold, I will take the people of Israel from the nations among which they have gone, and will gather them from all sides, and bring them to their own land; and I will make them one nation in the land, upon the mountains of Israel; and one king shall be king over them all; and they shall be no longer two nations, and no longer divided into two kingdoms. They shall not defile themselves any more with their idols and their detestable things, or with any of their transgressions; but I will save them from all the backslidings in which they have sinned, and will cleanse them; and they shall be my people, and I will be

their God. '*My servant David shall be king over them; and they shall all have one shepherd. They shall follow my ordinances and be careful to observe my statutes. They shall dwell in the land where your fathers dwelt that I gave to my servant Jacob; they and their children and their children's children shall dwell there for ever; and David my servant shall be their prince for ever.*" (Ezek. 37:21-25) "*Therefore, behold, I will allure her, and bring her into the wilderness, and speak tenderly to her. And there I will give her vineyards, and make the Valley of Achor a door of hope. And there she shall answer as in the days of her youth, as at the time when she came out of the land of Egypt. 'And in that day, says the LORD, you will call me, 'My husband,' and no longer will you call me, 'My Baal.'*" (Hosea 2:14-16)*

"*And the LORD said to me, 'Go again, love a woman who is beloved of a paramour and is an adulteress; even as the LORD loves the people of Israel, though they turn to other gods and love cakes of raisins.' So I bought her for fifteen shekels of silver and a homer and a lethech of barley. And I said to her, 'You must dwell as mine for many days; you shall not play the harlot, or belong to another man; so, will I also be to you.' For the children of Israel shall dwell many days without king or prince, without sacrifice or pillar, without ephod or teraphim. Afterward the children of Israel shall return and seek the LORD their God, and David their king; and they shall come in fear to the LORD and to his goodness in the latter days.*" (Hosea 3)

"*The LORD will have compassion on Jacob and will again choose Israel, and will set them in their own land, and aliens will join them and will cleave to the house of Jacob. And the peoples will take them and bring them to their place, and the house of Israel will possess them in the LORD's land as male and female slaves; they will take captive those who were their captors, and rule over those who oppressed them.*" (Isa. 14:1,2)

111

"For behold, in those days and at that time, when I restore the fortunes of Judah and Jerusalem, I will gather all the nations and bring them down to the valley of Jehoshaphat, and I will enter into judgment with them there, on account of my people and my heritage Israel, because they have scattered them among the nations, and have divided up my land, and have cast lots for my people, and have given a boy for a harlot, and have sold a girl for wine, and have drunk it. 'What are you to me, O Tyre and Sidon, and all the regions of Philistia? Are you paying me back for something? If you are paying me back, I will requite your deed upon your own head swiftly and speedily. For you have taken my silver and my gold and have carried my rich treasures into your temples. You have sold the people of Judah and Jerusalem to the Greeks, removing them far from their own border. But now I will stir them up from the place to which you have sold them, and I will requite your deed upon your own head. I will sell your sons and your daughters into the hand of the sons of Judah, and they will sell them to the Sabeans, to a nation far off; for the LORD has spoken." (Joel 3:1-8)

"In that day I will raise up the booth of David that is fallen and repair its breaches, and raise up its ruins, and rebuild it as in the days of old; that they may possess the remnant of Edom and all the nations who are called by my name,' says the LORD who does this. 'Behold, the days are coming,' says the LORD, 'when the plowman shall overtake the reaper and the treader of grapes him who sows the seed; the mountains shall drip sweet wine, and all the hills shall flow with it. I will restore the fortunes of my people Israel, and they shall rebuild the ruined cities and inhabit them; they shall plant vineyards and drink their wine, and they shall make gardens and eat their fruit. I will plant them upon their land, and they shall never again be plucked up out of the land which I have given them,' says the LORD your God." (Amos 9:11-15)

VII. The Davidic Covenant

Features (1) a temple in Israel, (2) a kingdom in perpetuity, (3) a throne, i.e., royal authority in the line of David, and (4) chastisement on sons for their disobedience. The promise of Messiah in the line of David is confirmed.

"Now therefore thus you shall say to my servant David, 'Thus says the LORD of hosts, I took you from the pasture, from following the sheep, that you should be prince over my people Israel; and I have been with you wherever you went, and have cut off all your enemies from before you; and I will make for you a great name, like the name of the great ones of the earth. And I will appoint a place for my people Israel, and will plant them, that they may dwell in their own place, and be disturbed no more; and violent men shall afflict them no more, as formerly, from the time that I appointed judges over my people Israel; and I will give you rest from all your enemies. Moreover, the LORD declares to you that the LORD will make you a house. When your days are fulfilled and you lie down with your fathers, I will raise up your offspring after you, who shall come forth from your body, and I will establish his kingdom. He shall build a house for my name, and I will establish the throne of his kingdom for ever. I will be his father, and he shall be my son. When he commits iniquity, I will chasten him with the rod of men, with the stripes of the sons of men; but I will not take my steadfast love from him, as I took it from Saul, whom I put away from before you, and your house and your kingdom shall be made sure for ever before me; your throne shall be established forever.'" (2 Sam. 7:8-16)

"Therefore, the Lord says, the LORD of hosts, the Mighty One of Israel: 'Ah, I will vent my wrath on my enemies, and avenge myself on my foes. I will turn my hand against you and will smelt away your dross as with lye and remove all your alloy. And I

113

will restore your judges as at the first, and your counselors as at the beginning. Afterward you shall be called the city of righteousness, the faithful city.' Zion shall be redeemed by justice, and those in her who repent, by righteousness. But rebels and sinners shall be destroyed together, and those who forsake the LORD shall be consumed." (Isaiah 1:24-28)

"Thou hast said, 'I have made a covenant with my chosen one, I have sworn to David my servant: "I will establish your descendants forever and build your throne for all generations." [Selah] I have found David, my servant; with my holy oil I have anointed him; so that my hand shall ever abide with him, my arm also shall strengthen him. The enemy shall not outwit him, the wicked shall not humble him. I will crush his foes before him and strike down those who hate him. My faithfulness and my steadfast love shall be with him, and in my name shall his horn be exalted. I will set his hand on the sea and his right hand on the rivers. He shall cry to me, 'Thou art my Father, my God, and the Rock of my salvation.' And I will make him the first-born, the highest of the kings of the earth. My steadfast love I will keep for him for ever, and my covenant will stand firm for him. I will establish his line for ever and his throne as the days of the heavens. If his children forsake my law and do not walk according to my ordinances, if they violate my statutes and do not keep my commandments, then I will punish their transgression with the rod and their iniquity with scourges; but I will not remove from him my steadfast love, or be false to my faithfulness. I will not violate my covenant, or alter the word that went forth from my lips. Once for all I have sworn by my holiness; I will not lie to David. His line shall endure for ever, his throne as long as the sun before me. Like the moon it shall be established for ever; it shall stand firm while the skies endure." [Selah] (Psalm 89, excerpts)

VIII. The New Covenant

An everlasting, unconditional covenant imparting a renewed mind and heart to the recipients. Restored favor and blessing for Israel. Complete and final forgiveness and removal of sins. Indwelling of the Holy Spirit. A rebuilt temple in Israel (Ezek. 37:26,27a). Cessation of war and institution of world peace. The Greek word diatheke is used interchangeably 15 times in the New Testament for "covenant" and "testament."

"Now as they were eating, Jesus took bread, and blessed, and broke it, and gave it to the disciples and said, 'Take, eat; this is my body.' And he took a cup, and when he had given thanks he gave it to them, saying, 'Drink of it, all of you; for this is my blood of the covenant, which is poured out for many for the forgiveness of sins.'" (Matthew 26:26-28)

"Behold, the days are coming, says the LORD, when I will sow the house of Israel and the house of Judah with the seed of man and the seed of beast. And it shall come to pass that as I have watched over them to pluck up and break down, to overthrow, destroy, and bring evil, so I will watch over them to build and to plant, says the LORD. In those days they shall no longer say: 'The fathers have eaten sour grapes, and the children's teeth are set on edge.' But every one shall die for his own sin; each man who eats sour grapes, his teeth shall be set on edge. 'Behold, the days are coming, says the LORD, when I will make a new covenant with the house of Israel and the house of Judah, not like the covenant which I made with their fathers when I took them by the hand to bring them out of the land of Egypt, my covenant which they broke, though I was their husband, says the LORD.

"But this is the covenant which I will make with the house of Israel after those days, says the LORD: I will put my law within

them, and I will write it upon their hearts; and I will be their God, and they shall be my people. And no longer shall each man teach his neighbor and each his brother, saying, `Know the LORD,' for they shall all know me, from the least of them to the greatest, says the LORD; for I will forgive their iniquity, and I will remember their sin no more.' Thus says the LORD, who gives the sun for light by day and the fixed order of the moon and the stars for light by night, who stirs up the sea so that its waves roar—the LORD of hosts is his name: 'If this fixed order departs from before me, says the LORD, then shall the descendants of Israel cease from being a nation before me for ever.' Thus says the LORD: 'If the heavens above can be measured, and the foundations of the earth below can be explored, then I will cast off all the descendants of Israel for all that they have done, says the LORD.' 'Behold, the days are coming, says the LORD, when the city shall be rebuilt for the LORD from the tower of Hananel to the Corner Gate. And the measuring line shall go out farther, straight to the hill Gareb, and shall then turn to Goah. The whole valley of the dead bodies and the ashes, and all the fields as far as the brook Kidron, to the corner of the Horse Gate toward the east, shall be sacred to the LORD. It shall not be uprooted or overthrown any more for ever." (Jer. 31)

"But as it is, Christ has obtained a ministry which is as much more excellent than the old as the covenant he mediates is better, since it is enacted on better promises. For if that first covenant had been faultless, there would have been no occasion for a second. For he finds fault with them when he says: 'The days will come, says the Lord, when I will establish a new covenant with the house of Israel and with the house of Judah; not like the covenant that I made with their fathers on the day when I took them by the hand to lead them out of the land of Egypt; for they did not continue in my covenant, and so I paid no heed to them, says the Lord. This is the covenant that I will make with the house of Israel after those

days, says the Lord: I will put my laws into their minds, and write them on their hearts, and I will be their God, and they shall be my people. And they shall not teach every one his fellow or every one his brother, saying, 'Know the Lord,' for all shall know me, from the least of them to the greatest. For I will be merciful toward their iniquities, and I will remember their sins no more.' In speaking of a new covenant he treats the first as obsolete. And what is becoming obsolete and growing old is ready to vanish away." (Heb. 8:8-13)

CHAPTER 16

Forgiveness

The perfect love of God that casts out all fear, the love in which we are to walk in the power of the Holy Spirit, will never operate in us, if we harbor any anger or bitterness toward any person or situation from the past or occurring now. Everyone has been hurt or offended by someone or something in the past and has some unbearable burden of resentment that only Jesus can lift from his shoulders. Jesus has forgiven and taken away all sin, sickness and disease, but His power to answer prayer and perform miracles that we pray for is completely blocked by any enmity, anger or resentment that you cling to refusing to forgive.

> *1 Corinthians 13:4-10*
> *Love suffers long and is kind; love does not envy; love does not parade itself, is not puffed up; does not behave rudely, does not seek its own, is not provoked, thinks no evil; does not rejoice in iniquity, but rejoices in the truth; bears all things, believes all things, hopes all things, endures all things.*
> *Love never fails. But whether there are prophecies, they will fail; whether there are tongues, they will cease; whether there is knowledge, it will vanish away. For we know in part and we prophesy in part. ¹⁰But when that which is perfect has come, then that which is in part will be done away?*

Much prayer of believers seems to go unanswered not because of doubt or unbelief, but because of unforgiveness that has hardened the heart to such a point that the Holy Spirit cannot penetrate its stony walls to receive fulfillment or the manifestation of anything Godly. Indeed, Jesus stands at the door and knocks and will come in and give you rest, but if that door in you is so tightly locked down in stone, you will always miss that knock and remain infantile in your faith. You will also be ready bait for Satan and his demons as you fail continually to receive answers to prayer. If you know and believe all scripture and still have no response to prayer, it is you and not Satan, a demon or your mother-in-law who is the cause; it is you and the hardness of your heart that are the cause.

There are many other causes of disappointment such as continuing in sin, holding onto unsavory companions or sex partners outside of wedlock, various addictions and false beliefs or doctrines, but as soon as any sincere prayer to the Father in the name of His only begotten Son Jesus Christ is uttered it is granted, though its fulfillment may be delayed for months, years or decades by the obstacles in your own heart. When those obstacles first arise in you they may be easy to recognize and to purge from your heart. But when they become entrenched within you for many years, they become more and more difficult to change. Either way no man can cleanse his own heart without the help of Jesus and the Holy Spirit.

Very often those who finally seek God's help to conquer and escape from their own hatred and anger and unforgiveness start to receive answer to prayer long forgotten. Their eyes are opened and their ears unstopped to receive long awaited revelation, wisdom and understanding from which they had blinded their own eyes.

> *Matthew 6:14-15*
> *"For if you forgive men their trespasses, your heavenly Father will also forgive you. But if you do not forgive men their trespasses, neither will your Father forgive your trespasses.*

These two verses following the Lord's Prayer are the ones never recited in churches and the preceding prayer is mumbled through at church by most Christians as ritual with no awareness of what is being said or its meaning.

Jesus was instructing His disciples how to pray in his miraculously brief but all-inclusive outline. *"Our Father"* refers to the Father of our Lord Jesus Christ, our Savior by Whom He created the universe and the Father of all of us who believe on His Son. *"Who art in heaven"* locates His abode and the eternal abode of Christ and all believers who are joint heirs with Him.

"Hallowed be thy name" instructs His disciples and us in a single word how to regard God when we pray to Him, whereas there are not enough words to express how He should be hallowed, revered, exalted, honored, lauded, glorified, etc. *"Give us this day our daily bread"* includes in the petition multitudes of things: our bread and water of life in the word, our bread and wine of communion with Christ, our physical sustenance, the blood of Jesus by which we were healed and saved, provision of all material thing that we need and infinitely more than can be named

"Forgive us our trespasses, as we forgive those who trespass against us", otherwise translated, *"forgive us our debts as we*

forgive our debtors."; Jesus knew that by our human, carnal nature our first plea would be for our own forgiveness before we would mention our forgiveness for our debtors. Though God's love for us is unconditional, He did make His forgiving us dependent upon our forgiveness of others. We can't qualify to 'be holy as He is holy until we can forgive as He forgives all offenses and unpaid monetary debts. Only with the Holy Spirit's help can the new born creature in us forgive completely as Christ forgives and attain holiness.by the mind of Christ.

"Lead us not into temptation but deliver us from evil" covers protection from our own carnal lusts, the enticements of the world and the wiles of the devil.

"For Thine is the kingdom, the power and the glory' makes emphatically clear that Satan's kingdom of darkness has no more dominion or authority in the earth, nor any power that can stand against God's eternal kingdom of light in which all glory abides

> *Matthew 18:21-35*
> *Then Peter came to Him and said, "Lord, how often shall my brother sin against me, and I forgive him? Up to seven times?"*
> *Jesus said to him, "I do not say to you, up to seven times, but up to seventy times seven. Therefore, the kingdom of heaven is like a certain king who wanted to settle accounts with his servants. ⁴And when he had begun to settle accounts, one was brought to him who owed him ten thousand talents. But as he was not able to pay, his master commanded that he be sold, with his wife and children and all that he had, and that payment be made. The servant therefore fell down before him, saying, 'Master, have patience with me, and I will pay*

you all.' Then the master of that servant was moved with compassion, released him, and forgave him the debt.

"But that servant went out and found one of his fellow servants who owed him a hundred denarii; and he laid hands on him and took him by the throat, saying, 'Pay me what you owe!' So his fellow servant fell down at his feet[d] and begged him, saying, 'Have patience with me, and I will pay you all.' And he would not, but went and threw him into prison till he should pay the debt. [31] So when his fellow servants saw what had been done, they were very grieved, and came and told their master all that had been done. Then his master, after he had called him, said to him, 'You wicked servant! I forgave you all that debt because you begged me. Should you not also have had compassion on your fellow servant, just as I had pity on you?' And his master was angry, and delivered him to the torturers until he should pay all that was due to him.

"So My heavenly Father also will do to you if each of you, from his heart, does not forgive his brother his trespasses."[

CHAPTER 17

Deliverance

In these end times, when all prophesied signs of the Lord's coming are either manifest or initiated, the attacks of the devil upon mankind in the form of multiple addictions, lusts and illnesses have intensified, as Satan knows that his time is short and that he is soon to be cast down to earth for a few years and then into the lake of fire to burn in torment forever in the lake of fire.

> Revelation 20:10
> The devil, who deceived them, was cast into the lake of fire
> and brimstone where the beast and the false prophet are.
> And they will be tormented day and night forever and ever.

We are all at some time in our lives enslaved to something because of the sinful nature into which we were born, and all need redemption from Jesus Christ in order to become free from that powerful sinful nature. There are those of us who are simply unaware of or deliberately oblivious of our sinful nature and others who embrace that nature enthusiastically.

There is no greater or lesser degree of sinfulness and all have sinned and fallen short of the glory of God, for which Jesus has qualified all of us who merely repent and believe and seek Him. Satan is fond of confusing and deceiving believers with a long list of sins that can be committed, whereas the scriptures give us no list, since there is only one sin, and that is to do anything that is contrary to the will of God. There is only one place to learn what is the will of God, and if you seek in the Scriptures, where it is found, you will find not only His will but also The Holy Spirit to reveal it to you.

> *Romans 6:16*
> *Do you not know that to whom you present yourselves*
> *slaves to obey, you are that one's slaves whom you obey,*
> *whether of sin leading to death, or of obedience leading*
> *to righteousness?*

All need repentance, that is, to turn away from sin and sin no more, however, all also need deliverance and liberation from sin and the only one who can provide deliverance from any and all enslaving sin is our Lord Jesus Christ. The devil uses all that we see in society around us to deceive us into thinking that only the most abominable criminals need repentance and only the most incorrigible addicts need deliverance, but in reality, you and I too also need both repentance and deliverance.

The heinous crimes for which the natural man in human society does not and can not forgive his fellow man, God has forgiven and taken away with all the rest of the sin of the world on His cross. No one convicted by human society or government and sitting on death row or in prison for life for his crimes can ever be separated from the love of God and his salvation by the blood of Christ when he repents, confesses in his heart and before men and believes that Jesus Christ is his Lord and redeemer.

Until we are able to receive that fullness of God's love into our heart's and act as His vessels to dispense it to the world, we fall short of His holiness and remain in need of repentance and deliverance, deliverance from our prejudice and judgment.

> *Romans 12:19*
> *Beloved, do not avenge yourselves, but rather give place to wrath; for it is written, "Vengeance is Mine, I will repay," says the Lord.*

It is not the vilest criminal, however, who is in greatest danger of missing salvation and going to hell; it is rather the reputable citizen never convicted or accused of anything who has managed to conceal his sin from all but God and foolishly imagines that God too has not perceived it. Far too many upright citizens in that position merely fail to repent and ask to receive the Lord as savior because they think themselves adequately virtuous to qualify for heaven, which they accept intellectually without any knowledge of Scripture or spiritual revelation. The egregious sinner, however knows that he is a sinner and is more likely to know how much he needs justification and salvation.

The seeker of deliverance must tread very cautiously and be determined and prepared for a rough battle between his flesh and his spirit, one that may take a long time and gradual progress with occasional setbacks, some perhaps all the way back to bondage. When Satan holds you in his grip he is relatively unconcerned, but when he loses you he will do his worst to get you back.

Luke 11:24-25

"When an unclean spirit goes out of a man, he goes through dry places, seeking rest; and finding none, he says, 'I will return to my house from which I came.' And when he comes, he finds it swept and put in order. Then he goes and takes with him seven other spirits more wicked than himself, and they enter and dwell there; and the last state of that man is worse than the first."

To triumph in this battle, you will need total commitment, persistence and determination, qualities which you have probably not exercised. What you lack, however, Jesus will supply, but you must avail yourself of it all and put on the full armor of God to stand.

Ephesians 6:10-18

Finally, my brethren, be strong in the Lord and in the power of His might. Put on the whole armor of God, that you may be able to stand against the wiles of the devil. For we do not wrestle against flesh and blood, but against principalities, against powers, against the rulers of the darkness of this age] against spiritual hosts of wickedness in the heavenly places. Therefore, take up the whole armor of God, that you may be able to withstand in the evil day, and having done all, to stand. Stand therefore, having girded your waist with truth, having put on the breastplate of righteousness, and having shod your feet with the preparation of the gospel of peace; above all, taking the shield of faith with which you will be able to quench all the fiery darts of the wicked one. And take the helmet of salvation, and the sword of the Spirit, which is the word of God; praying always with all prayer and supplication in the Spirit, being watchful to this end with all perseverance and supplication for all the saints"

All of these weapons are spiritual weapons, and there is no need to run around to various antique dealers looking for their physical counterparts as some rather foolish Christians have actually done. The battle, in any case is the Lord's, and as important as all this spiritual gear is, the essential part is "praying always with all prayer and supplication in the Spirit." The apostle Paul also says, *"Pray without ceasing."*

1 Thessalonians 5:16-18
Rejoice always, [17]pray without ceasing, in everything give thanks; for this is the will of God in Christ Jesus for you.

Joy is one of the precious fruits of the Spirit against which we can all measure our spiritual health, but the golden gate through which we gain access to all of them is giving thanks not only for what we have, but more so for all that we pray and hope for before seeing it manifest. Deliverance requires profoundly sincere thanks for the things hoped for.

Galatians 5:21-25
But the fruit of the Spirit is love, joy, peace, longsuffering, kindness, goodness, faithfulness, gentleness, self-control. Against such there is no law. And those who are Christ's have crucified the flesh with its passions and desires. If we live in the Spirit, let us also walk in the Spirit.

Psalm 100:4-5
Enter into His gates with thanksgiving, And into His courts with praise.

Be thankful to Him, and bless His name.
For the LORD is good; His mercy is everlasting, And
His truth endures to all generations.

Psalm 97
It is good to give thanks to the LORD,
And to sing praises to Your name, O Most High;
To declare Your lovingkindness in the morning, And
Your faithfulness every night,
³On an instrument of ten strings, On the lute,
And on the harp,
With harmonious sound.
For You, LORD, have made me glad through Your
work; I will triumph in the works of Your hands.
O LORD, how great are Your works! Your thoughts
are very deep.
A senseless man does not know, Nor does a fool
understand this.
When the wicked spring up like grass,
And when all the workers of iniquity flourish, It is that
they may be destroyed forever.
But You, LORD, are on high forevermore.
For behold, Your enemies, O LORD, For behold, Your
enemies shall perish;
All the workers of iniquity shall be scattered.
But my horn You have exalted like a wild ox; I have
been anointed with fresh oil.
My eye also has seen my desire on my enemies; My ears
hear my desire on the wicked
Who rise up against me.
The righteous shall flourish like a palm tree, He shall
grow like a cedar in Lebanon.
Those who are planted in the house of the LORD Shall
flourish in the courts of our God.

They shall still bear fruit in old age;
To declare that the LORD is upright;
He is my rock, and there is no unrighteousness
in Him.

Deliverance From Sexual Sin

Repentance must be at the threshold of every door to deliverance from anything to which one has become enslaved. There is nobody who has not committed some kind of sexual sin, because sex is the realm in which our sinful nature has the tightest hold on us. Jesus has taken all of that sin on the cross with Him and forgiven it to all who repent and ask Him. But there are many who are possessed by some form of sexual sin, whose deliverance is just as easily achieved by repentance but very difficult to be freed from.

Jesus made clear what was not required or understood in the law of Moses that adultery involves more spiritual damage than the adulterous act.

> *Matthew 5:27-28*
> *"You have heard that it was said to those of old,[l] 'You shall not commit adultery.' 8But I say to you that whoever looks at a woman to lust for her has already committed adultery with her in his heart.*

What Jesus says here applies to all things sexual that can corrupt the heart, and theological limitation of its application exclusively to married men lusting after women and single men lusting after married women is a misinterpretation. This scripture applies to all sexual lust of every kind, heterosexual or homosexual and in holy matrimony or out.

Properly married couples are themselves in adultery when sexual lust is the sole foundation of their marriage. That is why divorce is so prevalent; those marriages founded on anything other than the God ordained model established in the book of Genesis is vulnerable to failure.

> *Genesis 2:24*
> *Therefore a man shall leave his father and mother and*
> *be joined to his wife, and they shall become one flesh.*

This model for marriage is the only Biblical model that conforms with the will of God, and it is reiterated many times throughout the Scriptures. The current dilemma in denominational churches and various theological schools of thought over homosexuality, ordination of homosexuals, homosexual marriage, hatred of homosexuals, excommunication of homosexuals, etc. is mostly mishandled because of erroneous man-made doctrines that do not derive from Scripture. The clear scriptural mandate in this regard is that

1. God's love is unconditional toward all who draw breath.
2. Homosexuality is contrary to the plan and the will of God, and thus must be called sin.

a) *Romans 1:18-27*
   For the wrath of God is revealed from heaven against all
   ungodliness and unrighteousness of men, who suppress
   the truth in unrighteousness, because what may be
   known of God is manifest in them, for God has shown it
   to them. For since the creation of the world His invisible

attributes are clearly seen, being understood by the things that are made, even His eternal power and Godhead, so that they are without excuse, because, although they knew God, they did not glorify Him as God, nor were thankful, but became futile in their thoughts, and their foolish hearts were darkened. Professing to be wise, they became fools, and changed the glory of the incorruptible God into an image made like corruptible man—and birds and four-footed animals and creeping things.

Therefore God also gave them up to uncleanness, in the lusts of their hearts, to dishonor their bodies among themselves, who exchanged the truth of God for the lie, and worshiped and served the creature rather than the Creator, who is blessed forever. Amen.

For this reason, God gave them up to vile passions. For even their women exchanged the natural use for what is against nature. Likewise also the men, leaving the natural use of the woman, burned in their lust for one another, men with men committing what is shameful, and receiving in themselves the penalty of their error which was due.

This part of Romans 1 firmly establishes that homosexuality is lust of the flesh like any other lust of the flesh, heterosexual or bestial, and thus sin.

It is the next part of the scripture that enrages and alienates homosexuals.

Romans 1:28-
For the wrath of God is revealed from heaven against all ungodliness and unrighteousness of men, who suppress the truth in unrighteousness, because what may be known of God is manifest in them, for God has shown it to them. For since the creation of the world His invisible

attributes are clearly seen, being understood by the things that are made, even His eternal power and Godhead, so that they are without excuse, because, although they knew God, they did not glorify Him as God, nor were thankful, but became futile in their thoughts, and their foolish hearts were darkened. Professing to be wise, they became fools, and changed the glory of the incorruptible God into an image made like corruptible man—and birds and four-footed animals and creeping things.

Therefore God also gave them up to uncleanness, in the lusts of their hearts, to dishonor their bodies among themselves, ²⁵who exchanged the truth of God for the lie, and worshiped and served the creature rather than the Creator, who is blessed forever. Amen.

²⁶For this reason God gave them up to vile passions. For even their women exchanged the natural use for what is against nature. ²⁷Likewise also the men, leaving the natural use of the woman, burned in their lust for one another, men with men committing what is shameful, and receiving in themselves the penalty of their error which was due.

It is self-evident that no one living in homosexual sin could possibly welcome the multiplicity of seeming condemnations against him, but he who condemns and throws the first stone sins perhaps more gravely than the accused, because it is not our province to judge. We have an adequate judge who will also judge us. It is rather our province to love the sinner with the unconditional love of Jesus and to bring him to repentance. No man or woman ever stood accused of each and every one of the evils mentioned in Romans 1, but it is Satan who is the accuser, and who by his accusation hopes to entrap the sinner in his sin. Jesus has won the victory over the devil two thousand years ago and has deliverance and redemption for all who have sinned. Believers must embrace recovering homosexuals just as they do the poor, the homeless and recovering drug addicts. Jesus' perfect love casts out all fear one of another or of any wiles of the devil.

Deliverance from Alcohol and Drug Addiction

The one formula for deliverance from anything is the same single formula as that for justification and salvation: Jesus Christ. The only difference between sexual immorality and drug addiction is that the role of choice is more obvious. God's grace can break any addiction when one makes the choice. It is your bad choice that has left you addicted, but the love of Jesus and His blood on the cross can also take away all your bad choices even though you have corrupted and damaged your body, which is the temple of His Holy Spirit.

In addiction you surrender your body to toxic substances that are lethal and give no warning when they will kill you; they are substances that make you feel good up to that final moment or the moment when they will strike you crippled for life, and their chemical hold on all your bodily functions will not release you without extensive detoxification, whose results are not likely to be permanent. Also, if you get off one drug, the devil has another stronger one ready for you, and there is no end to the downward roller coaster but death. Satan has developed such a perfect automated system to kill you that no human intervention can stop him.

Only Jesus Christ our Lord has triumphed over all these substances to provide deliverance from their power and even to heal all your self-inflicted damage to the body and the mind. If you have once been delivered and fallen away, the lord will never leave you and forsake you when all of your family and friends have done so. He will pick you up and forgive your failure and keep your name written in the Lamb's book of life when you repent.

Deliverance from Anger, Violence and Unforgiveness

If you have a problem with anger or an always combative nature, ready to seek a fight on all sides and hold lifetime grudges, there is no need to claim that to be your nature that nothing can change. All of that is merely sin that you cling to by choice, and it is destroying your life. If you will make the firm, sincere decision to change, the Holy Spirit will deliver you from anger with your wife and children and any propensity you might have to beat or abuse them. He can also keep you from losing jobs and having to flee constantly from the law because of your temper. God has forgiveness and deliverance for both the perpetrator of violence and the victim who believes and asks for it, for God loves them both.

CHAPTER 18
Eternal Life in Resurrection

June 17, 2011 in mid–afternoon when I was quite fatigued. I decided to go out to a nearby lake across from which was a Dairy Queen. I felt that the preceding chapters were completed in draft prior to proof reading on it would be refreshing to have an ice cream cone. I crossed over the busy street at the clearly marked crosswalk and bought the cone. Then I immediately started to cross back over to the lake side without yet having even tasted the cone. Alas, I never made it to the other side, because an elderly woman drove her car into me at forty miles an hour. The electric wheelchair in which I was crossing was demolished and my body hurled about thirty feet down the pavement, stripped of all garments and consciousness. Upon impact I had time for only one ridiculously trivial conscious thought; nothing concerned with death or heaven or hell; the single thought was regret that I had not been able to take a single lick at that ice cream cone.

I was taken by ambulance to a major hospital emergency room where the doctors gave me no chance of survival. I learned upon gaining consciousness they left me for hours on the board from the ambulance on which I had been delivered because they had expected to carry me out on it to the morgue. When I failed to expire as quickly as they had expected they put me in a bed in intensive care where they kept me for about five days, still expecting my demise. I had to inquire about all that happened subsequently for about two weeks because I was kept unconscious under sedation to mitigate my writhing and moaning in pain while many bone fractures of my legs and pelvis were being set.

Whether I died or not I don't know. It was certainly not I who consciously did all the many things that were reported to me about my actions for the first two weeks in the hospital. It is the Holy Spirit who took charge of my tongue to pray loudly for me in tongues, my holy prayer language which He had given me in 1954 through baptism in the Holy Spirit. Though my body was showing life signs the entire time and it is reported to have exhibited severe pain, my spirit was initially unaware of it. I don't know whether I was still in the body at the time. At any rate, upon regaining consciousness I continued praying in tongues every waking moment. At the same time, I was covered with an incessant blanket of prayer by pastors and brothers and sisters in Christ from my church congregation.

The one brother who did the most is Pr. Michael Hyland, a confirmed night owl who was praying at my bedside almost every night for two to four hours anywhere between midnight and four o'clock in the morning. He is the one who was able to tell me most about what happened. It was the Lord who provided him for me, but there are countless other miraculous things that He provided. The police arrived very quickly and found the phone number of my church in my wallet that was tucked into the rear pocket of my wheelchair lying demolished all over the pavement. They called the number and were able to report the accident. Nobody was scheduled to be at that number at that time, but the Lord arranged that pastor Pamela, quite unusually, happened to be in the office preparing a lesson, and she answered the phone. Normally she would never answer that phone; she would leave that for the church secretary. Then she immediately called Pr. Greg Giacomini, who could normally not be reached during a work day. Nevertheless, he arrived at the emergency room before my ambulance did. He stayed and prayed for me until Mike arrived to take over.

Though many people think it possible that such an accident might be caused by God to punish some kind of sin, nothing could be further from the truth and a lie from the pit of hell. God in His infinite wisdom indeed knew that the accident would happen and that Satan caused it and meant it to destroy me, but God turned it around into a great blessing, both to bless me and to glorify His name. Not only did he send an angel to prevent me from suffering spinal damage, whiplash, concussion and multiple internal injuries, but he sent another to read scriptures to me for hours in the middle of the night one evening just after my regaining consciousness when Mike could not come. The reader was dressed as a doctor with a stethoscope around his neck. He did not examine me or inquire about my condition; he only sat down by the bed and asked if I would like to have him read and pray for me. I never learned who he was nor saw him again. He had read all of Romans, Galatians and Ephesians to me.

Many people have seen and described their near-death experiences ether in heaven or sinking into hell. I cannot, however, describe any such experience, because I did not go through such things myself, and cannot draw any analogies from their experiences. What I do know, however, is that the Holy Spirit acted powerfully on my behalf when I was near death and incapable of even asking for help. The one thing that I can tell with certainty is that despite my decades of apostasy the Lord was not going to let me go or to forsake me as I deserved. Though my zeal was reignited in 1998, and I repented of allowing the world, the flesh and the devil to make me drift so far from the perfect will of God so long. There is no kind of merit in my belated new repentance except the glory, God's miraculous glory that he manifested in his faithfulness. He only magnified His grace toward me and expanded the scope of His favor that I enjoyed from earliest childhood and had never deserved an only very late in life thanked Him for. He even left me in better general health than I had had before the accident.

The Father, the Son and the Holy Spirit have the same limitless love and favor for you that they have manifested toward me, because you are God's favorite as much as or more than I am. Just as He has provided to me free of charge all the qualifications required to walk now, while still on earth in the flesh, in eternal life (on earth as it is in heaven), He has the same stored up for you whenever you ask and thank Him for it. There is no need for anyone to be cast with Satan into the pit of hell nor to barely make it across the threshold of heaven with scant inheritance, because it is the perfect will of God that none should perish, but that all might have eternal life.

Praise His holy name!!!

Other Works Soon Available
By Bruce Bullock

Mysteries of God

2 novellas
Reconciled Post Mortem

Inmate Confined for Jesus
   Story of a redemption